The Menendez Brothers' Untold Story

Family Secrets, Tragic Loss, and the Journey from Conviction to an Emotional Reunion After Years Apart

David shaun s.

Dedication

To those who embrace life with humor, resilience, and an open heart—

and to everyone who has ever found courage in laughter. This book is dedicated to Teri Garr's family, friends, and fans, who continue to carry her light forward. May her spirit inspire you, her laughter uplift you, and her story remind you that even in the face of life's challenges, joy and strength are always within reach. Thank you, Teri, for the laughter and the legacy.

Copyright

Table of content

Table of Contents

Introduction

The Menendez Brothers: A Brief Overview

The Menendez brothers, Lyle and Erik, are names that became etched in the collective memory of America, not for achievements or accolades, but for a crime that would haunt the nation. On a warm August night in 1989, their parents, José and Kitty Menendez, were brutally murdered in their Beverly Hills mansion, sending shockwaves across the country. What began as a sensational news story, marked by the gruesome nature of the crime, soon transformed into a deeply complex tale of family, power, and alleged abuse that divided public opinion for decades. Lyle, the older of the two, was 21 at the time, known for his sharp mind and ambition that mirrored his father's. Erik, just 18, was more reserved, often seen as the sensitive one, struggling under the weight of both family expectations and his father's overbearing presence. To outsiders, the brothers were heirs to a successful family, enjoying the privileges of wealth and influence. They had grown up surrounded by all the symbols of success—the Beverly Hills address, elite schools, and promising futures. But behind the carefully crafted facade, their lives were anything but idyllic.

The murder investigation that followed was filled with twists and turns that captivated the public. At first, the brothers were not even suspects. They appeared to be grieving sons, devastated by the tragic loss of their parents. However, as details emerged, questions began to arise. How could these young men, seemingly in shock, so quickly turn to spending their inheritance on luxury items and personal indulgences? Their lavish purchases—a Rolex for Lyle, a tennis coach for Erik, trips, cars, and other extravagances—soon fueled suspicion, casting them in a different light.

In the ensuing trial, the brothers' defense brought forward allegations of severe emotional and sexual abuse at the hands of their father, which they claimed had pushed them to commit the murders out of fear and desperation. The narrative shifted yet again, painting a darker, more nuanced picture of life inside the Menendez home. José, once seen as the hard-driving, successful patriarch, was now depicted as a tyrant, whose relentless ambition extended into every corner of his family life, while Kitty was portrayed as a passive, sometimes neglectful figure, unable to shield her sons from the alleged horrors they endured.

As the case unfolded on national television, it became a public spectacle—a courtroom drama played out in front of millions. The first trial resulted in deadlocked juries, unable to decide if Lyle and Erik were calculating killers or deeply scarred victims of a traumatic upbringing. Their second trial, however, led to a conviction, sentencing both brothers to life without the possibility of parole. To some, justice had been served, while others questioned whether a tragic family history had been overlooked in favor of sensationalized justice.

Decades later, the Menendez brothers' story continues to evoke fascination, debate, and, in recent years, renewed sympathy as the understanding of familial abuse and trauma has evolved. Their case has been revisited through documentaries, podcasts, and even social media, with a new generation questioning whether the brothers' actions were rooted in survival rather than greed. With a recent push for resentencing, the Menendez brothers may once again have a chance to confront the justice system that sealed their fate so many years ago.

This brief overview only scratches the surface of a story layered with human complexity, a tale of family, betrayal, and the darkest corners of the human psyche. For many, Lyle and Erik Menendez are more than just convicted killers; they are symbols of a broken family, victims of their environment, and perhaps, in some ways, tragic figures in a society all too quick to judge.

Part I:

Family Background and Early Life

Chapter one

The Menendez Family

The Menendez family was not just a wealthy family; they were a living portrait of ambition, privilege, and the American Dream's glittering promise. In their luxurious Beverly Hills mansion, surrounded by signs of success, they appeared to outsiders as an ideal family: wealthy, accomplished, and complete. But like many polished exteriors, the Menendez household held secrets that simmered beneath the surface, bound by complicated dynamics that would eventually unravel in the most tragic way.

José Menendez: From Cuban Immigrant to Hollywood Executive

At the heart of this family's story was José Menendez, a man whose life was shaped by a journey marked by resilience, sacrifice, and a relentless desire to rise above his humble beginnings. Born in Havana, Cuba, José's early life was worlds away from the bright lights and affluence he would later embrace in America. Growing up in the political and economic turmoil of post-revolution Cuba, José witnessed firsthand the toll that instability and poverty could take on families. It was a life of scarcity, but even as a young boy, he dreamed of something more—something far beyond the reach of his modest circumstances.

When José was just a teenager, he left everything he knew, stepping onto American soil with little more than a fierce determination to succeed. He moved into his cousin's attic, working menial jobs and studying tirelessly, often late into the night, balancing dreams with the brutal reality of immigrant life. His ambition propelled him forward, from washing dishes to eventually earning a college scholarship for swimming. José was not content with merely surviving; he was driven by a vision that could only be realized by his unyielding work ethic and relentless pursuit of upward mobility.

It was during college that he met Mary Louise "Kitty" Anderson, a beauty pageant queen with a soft smile and an air of grace. For Kitty, José's confidence and relentless ambition were magnetic. He was unlike anyone she had ever met—intense, driven, and full of promise. Kitty, who had grown up in the modest comforts of small-town America, found herself drawn to this young man with grand dreams, a man who seemed destined to build a future that would lift them both to heights she had only imagined. They married and began their journey together, sharing a dream of wealth, status, and a family that would embody the success José worked so hard to achieve.

José's career took off quickly, a meteoric rise that transformed him from an immigrant with big dreams into a powerful executive in the entertainment industry. Starting with Hertz, he rose through the ranks, later becoming the head of RCA Records. In this role, he wasn't just another corporate figure; he was a tastemaker, playing a role in signing major acts like Duran Duran and Menudo, earning a reputation as a shrewd, formidable businessman with a touch of Hollywood flair. For José, this success was not just professional—it was personal validation, a testimony to how far he had come from his Cuban roots.

But with success came pressure, an intensity that seeped into every aspect of his life, including his family. José brought the same discipline and ambition to his household that he wielded in the boardroom. He wanted nothing less than excellence from his sons, Lyle and Erik, and he viewed them as reflections of his hard-won success. His relentless drive and high expectations defined his parenting style, leaving little room for mistakes, weaknesses, or rebellion. To him, failure was simply unacceptable; it was an affront to everything he had built and sacrificed.

Kitty, for her part, adjusted to life as the wife of a powerful executive, stepping into the role of a supportive partner and mother, although she often struggled to keep pace with José's unrelenting standards. The glamour of their lifestyle belied a deep vulnerability within her, as she tried to balance the demands of her husband's world with her own sense of self. The Menendez home, while outwardly a symbol of success, was becoming a pressure cooker, where ambition, expectation, and unspoken pain simmered quietly, unseen by the outside world but deeply felt by each family member.

Through José's eyes, the American Dream had been conquered, but beneath the surface, the cost was mounting. His boys were not merely sons; they were the legacy he intended to leave behind, the heirs to his dream and the standards he had set. Yet, in his relentless pursuit of perfection, José may have overlooked the delicate balance between discipline and compassion, ambition and acceptance. The Menendez family's story was one of undeniable success, but it was also one of deep, underlying tension—a household held together by pride, ambition, and expectations that would eventually lead to devastating consequences.

Kitty Menendez: A Life Behind the Glamour

Kitty Menendez was the quiet heart of the Menendez family, a woman whose life was shaped by the pursuit of stability and love, yet overshadowed by a sense of emptiness that even the wealth and prestige surrounding her could not fill. To outsiders, Kitty was the epitome of grace—a former beauty queen who had married into a life of luxury, moving from a modest Midwestern upbringing to the opulence of Beverly Hills. Yet behind her composed exterior, she was a woman who struggled to find her own identity amidst the intense world José had created.

Born Mary Louise Anderson, Kitty grew up in a small town, where life was simpler, if not exactly fulfilling. She was a beautiful, charming young woman, and her presence commanded attention wherever she went. Winning local beauty pageants gave her a taste of admiration and recognition, sparking dreams of a life that went beyond the boundaries of her quiet hometown. Like many young women of her time, Kitty grew up with visions of a fairy-tale marriage—a handsome, successful husband and a life adorned with the comforts that success could provide. Meeting José seemed like the fulfillment of that fantasy.

When she met José in college, he was everything she had hoped for and more. He was bold, ambitious, and driven by dreams of greatness that matched her own desire to escape the ordinary. Kitty found herself captivated by his passion and determination, and soon, her life became entwined with his relentless quest for success. She was not only marrying a man but joining a mission, a shared vision of rising to the highest echelons of society. As José's career skyrocketed, Kitty slipped into the role of the devoted wife, supporting him through the intense demands of his corporate climb.

Life in Beverly Hills seemed, on the surface, to offer everything Kitty had longed for. She had a beautiful home, social standing, and two sons she adored. But as the years passed, the glitter of her glamorous life began to dull. The truth was, the wealth and prestige that had once seemed like the ultimate goal turned out to be a gilded cage, trapping her in a world where appearances mattered more than authenticity. She was the wife of a powerful man, a role that required her to present a flawless front, yet beneath it all, she felt increasingly isolated and fragile.

Kitty's role in the family was that of the nurturer, the one who was meant to provide warmth and balance to José's intensity. But even in her maternal duties, she struggled. Kitty's own emotional battles with self-worth and depression often left her feeling detached from the sons she loved. Her relationship with Lyle and Erik was complex; she adored them deeply, yet often seemed distant, caught up in her own unspoken fears and disappointments. While José pushed the boys relentlessly toward his ideal of success, Kitty offered a softer, if inconsistent, form of love, one that was overshadowed by her own inner turmoil.

In private moments, Kitty grappled with the reality of her life—a life that, despite its outward perfection, felt increasingly hollow. She was surrounded by luxury, yet haunted by a sense of inadequacy that no amount of wealth could erase. Her marriage to José, while outwardly stable, was marked by a quiet suffering that she kept hidden from the world. José's affairs, his demanding nature, and his single-minded focus on control left little room for Kitty to find her own voice. She lived in his shadow, her own aspirations and needs stifled by the expectations of her role as the loyal, supportive wife.

The pressures of maintaining this perfect image began to take a toll on Kitty's mental health. She slipped into cycles of depression and substance abuse, using alcohol and prescription medications to numb the pain of a life that had drifted far from the dreams she once cherished. Her beauty and grace became masks she wore to conceal the cracks in her carefully constructed world. Inside, she was a woman who felt lost, trapped in a role that offered little solace and no escape.

Kitty's struggle was one of quiet desperation, a longing for a sense of purpose beyond the confines of her family's image. She had once believed in the promise of a beautiful life, but that promise had eroded, leaving behind a woman haunted by regrets and unfulfilled dreams. To those around her, Kitty Menendez was the elegant, supportive wife of a successful man, yet behind closed doors, she was a woman grasping for meaning in a life that had spun out of her control.

Chapter Two

The American Dream Meets Dysfunction

Moving to Beverly Hills: Power and Prestige

The move to Beverly Hills was, for the Menendez family, a moment that seemed to mark their arrival at the pinnacle of American success. For years, José had pursued every opportunity with a single-minded determination, transforming himself from an immigrant boy with dreams of a better life into a formidable figure in the entertainment industry. Now, with his wife Kitty and their two sons, he was stepping into the heart of luxury and influence—a world where fortunes and legacies were built, where celebrities and industry moguls lived side by side. Their new home in Beverly Hills wasn't just an address; it was a symbol of José's hard-won success, a public testament to how far he had come and, to some extent, what he believed his family was destined to represent.

Beverly Hills, with its manicured lawns, sprawling mansions, and a blend of old-world glamour and modern opulence, embodied the ideals that José had pursued since he first set foot in America. Moving there was not just a strategic decision but a statement—a way to place his family among the elite, reinforcing the image he had tirelessly crafted. The Menendez residence on Elm Drive sat in a neighborhood rich with history, the kind of place where each home told a story of wealth, ambition, and social prominence. This house, previously occupied by music legends and film icons, was yet another feather in José's cap, an achievement that showcased his rise from humble beginnings to a position of power and prestige.

For Kitty, Beverly Hills represented a dream come to life. She had long been accustomed to playing the role of the supportive spouse, standing by as José's career flourished, often at the cost of her own sense of identity. Now, she found herself in a setting that glittered with opportunity and status, a place where she could step into the role of the successful executive's wife with grace and elegance. The move was a chance for Kitty to embrace the social lifestyle she had once only imagined—attending charity galas, hosting gatherings, mingling with the wives of executives and celebrities. In many ways, Beverly Hills offered her an escape from the struggles of her past, a chance to reinvent herself amidst the palm trees and gated communities of Los Angeles' elite.

For Lyle and Erik, Beverly Hills offered both excitement and expectation. To the boys, the move meant new friends, new schools, and an entry into a lifestyle that would be the envy of most. But José's ambitions for his sons did not simply end with providing them access to luxury; he expected them to excel in this new environment, to carve out paths that would reflect the family's values of success, resilience, and superiority. Lyle, already a promising tennis player, and Erik, who had demonstrated his own athletic potential, were to embody José's vision of excellence, proving that the Menendez legacy would continue to rise.

Yet, behind the dazzling façade of Beverly Hills, cracks in the family's foundation were already forming. The demands of this lifestyle—the need to maintain appearances, to be the perfect family in the public eye—added pressure to an already strained household. José's drive for perfection extended into every aspect of their lives, leaving little room for flaws or failures. Kitty, who had hoped that this move might bring her a sense of fulfillment, instead found herself sinking into the shadows of José's unrelenting standards. Her own dreams and desires, so long stifled, were further buried beneath the image she was expected to uphold. The boys, too, felt the weight of their father's expectations in new and profound ways, as the pressure to succeed mounted with each passing day.

Life in Beverly Hills was both a blessing and a burden. For the Menendez family, it provided an elevated platform, a luxurious existence that many aspired to but few attained. Yet, in their home, hidden behind the closed doors of their mansion, the pursuit of power and prestige had fostered an atmosphere of quiet desperation. Each family member, in their own way, was grappling with the relentless pressure to uphold a facade that, while glittering on the outside, concealed an escalating tension within.

The American Dream, for the Menendez family, had indeed been achieved. But as they settled into their new life in Beverly Hills, it became increasingly clear that the dream came with a cost—one that would test their bonds, expose their vulnerabilities, and, ultimately, reveal the dysfunction festering beneath the surface. In their quest for success, they had reached a place of power and prestige, but in doing so, they were beginning to lose sight of the family they once were. Beverly Hills was a paradise of sorts, yet within its beauty lay the seeds of a tragedy that would one day shake their lives and capture the attention of the entire nation.

Parental Pressure: The Weight of Expectations on Lyle and Erik

For Lyle and Erik Menendez, life under their father's roof was an existence marked by intense expectation and an unyielding demand for excellence. In José's eyes, his sons were not just boys; they were the living embodiment of his legacy, the vessels through which his hard-won success would continue to thrive. He viewed their lives as extensions of his own ambitions, a chance to further validate the American Dream he had sacrificed so much to achieve. The move to Beverly Hills had only intensified his standards, elevating the family to a level where failure, in any form, was not an option.

Lyle, the elder son, bore the brunt of these expectations from an early age. José saw in Lyle a reflection of his own tenacity and intelligence, believing that his firstborn should follow closely in his footsteps. To José, Lyle's future was already mapped out, marked by high achievement in both academics and athletics. He was pushed relentlessly, especially on the tennis court, where José took an active role in managing every aspect of his training, setting goals that Lyle was expected to meet without question. Tennis, in José's mind, was not just a sport but a test of character, discipline, and determination—a proving ground that would shape Lyle into the man José wanted him to become.

While Lyle strove to meet his father's demands, he also felt a growing sense of suffocation. He wanted José's approval, craved it even, but the standards set for him seemed to move higher each time he reached them. No achievement was ever quite enough; victories were met with a nod, while shortcomings were dissected and scrutinized. The pressure to be perfect, to embody his father's vision, created an undercurrent of anxiety that Lyle struggled to manage. Over time, this pressure began to chip away at his self-confidence, replacing it with a simmering resentment—a feeling he dared not express, knowing the consequences of disappointing his father's relentless expectations.

For Erik, the weight of parental pressure took on a different shape. While Lyle faced José's expectations head-on, Erik internalized them, feeling the strain in a quieter but equally intense way. Naturally sensitive and introspective, Erik was not as outwardly driven as his older brother, yet he, too, was pushed to excel, particularly in tennis. José's involvement in Erik's athletic career was all-encompassing, managing every practice, scrutinizing every match, and ensuring that Erik adhered to a strict regimen. Success in tennis became synonymous with worth, and any deviation from this path was met with disappointment. For Erik, each match became a test, not just of skill, but of his value as his father's son.

José's influence permeated every aspect of Erik's life, leaving little room for personal desires or dreams that did not align with his father's vision. While Erik occasionally enjoyed the sport, his father's rigid demands transformed it into an obligation, a duty to fulfill rather than a passion to pursue. Unlike Lyle, who channeled his anxiety into a determined facade, Erik felt the weight of his father's expectations bearing down on him in quieter, more insidious ways. The constant drive to satisfy José's high standards left Erik struggling with self-doubt, a feeling that no matter how hard he tried, he would never be enough.

Kitty, though aware of her husband's intense pressure on the boys, often found herself powerless to intervene. She saw the toll that José's expectations were taking on Lyle and Erik, but she was caught in her own emotional battles, struggling with feelings of inadequacy and depression that left her distant and detached. Occasionally, she would attempt to shield her sons from José's harsh critiques, offering small gestures of encouragement, but her efforts were overshadowed by the dominant presence of her husband. In the Menendez home, José's voice was the law, and Kitty's attempts to soften his demands were often swept aside, leaving the boys to face the full force of their father's ambitions.

For both Lyle and Erik, life in the Menendez household was a delicate balancing act—a struggle to meet their father's relentless expectations while also navigating the desires and dreams they were forced to suppress. Their achievements were celebrated publicly, showcasing the family's status, but privately, there was an unspoken understanding that failure was unacceptable, that anything less than perfection was a reflection of weakness. The boys grew up under the constant gaze of a father who viewed them not as individuals but as extensions of his own legacy, bound to the trajectory he had meticulously crafted.

As they grew older, the toll of living under such scrutiny began to manifest in subtle but unmistakable ways. Lyle became more rebellious, finding ways to push back against his father's control, while Erik retreated inward, wrestling with a growing sense of anxiety that gnawed at his confidence. Both boys, in their own ways, felt trapped within the rigid expectations that defined their lives, yearning for a sense of freedom that seemed forever out of reach. They had become symbols of success, but at a cost that only they understood—a cost that would ultimately lead them down a path of resentment, desperation, and, finally, tragedy.

In the end, the Menendez brothers' story was shaped not just by the wealth and privilege they inherited, but by the crushing weight of expectations that came with it. Their father's dream of perfection, so deeply ingrained in every aspect of their lives, became a double-edged sword—a source of pride but also of unbearable pressure. And while they carried this burden with quiet resilience for years, it was only a matter of time before the weight of José's ambitions would push them beyond the point of endurance, setting the stage for the explosive events that would bring their family's hidden struggles to light for the entire world to see.

Cracks in the Facade: Signs of Strain and Rebellion

As the Menendez family settled into their life in Beverly Hills, outwardly projecting an image of success and unity, subtle cracks began to appear in the carefully constructed facade that José and Kitty had worked so hard to build. Beneath the surface of their seemingly perfect family, the strain of José's relentless expectations and the suffocating weight of a life defined by appearances started to manifest in both of their sons in troubling ways. Lyle and Erik, caught in the web of their father's ambition and their own unspoken resentment, began to rebel, each in his own way, as they struggled to reconcile their inner turmoil with the rigid standards imposed upon them.

For Lyle, the older of the two brothers, rebellion took the form of defiance cloaked in privilege. Raised to be the heir apparent to José's empire of success, Lyle knew what was expected of him—academic excellence, athletic prowess, and an unwavering commitment to the family's image. But the pressure to meet these standards eventually became too much. In a quiet act of defiance, he began to push the boundaries, testing his father's control in ways that were both subtle and overt. His early achievements in tennis were clouded by instances of reckless behavior, an indication that Lyle was beginning to chafe against the invisible chains of his father's expectations.

In high school and later at Princeton, Lyle's rebellious streak became more pronounced. Beneath the polished exterior of a young man destined for success, he began engaging in risky behavior. The culmination of his disobedience came when he was suspended from Princeton for plagiarism—a scandal that struck at the core of José's values. Plagiarism was, to José, a sign of weakness, a failure that represented not just a lapse in judgment but an insult to the disciplined, hardworking image he had crafted for his family. Rather than reprimanding Lyle in a way that might encourage reflection and personal growth, José responded with intense anger, using shame and guilt to try to reel his son back into line. This only served to deepen Lyle's resentment, pushing him further away emotionally and solidifying his quiet rebellion against his father's control.

Erik's path to rebellion was less direct but equally impactful. While Lyle's defiance was bold and outward, Erik's was quieter, a retreat into his own inner world. Unlike Lyle, who had learned to wear a mask of confidence, Erik was more vulnerable, more sensitive to the undercurrents of tension within their family. His early promise in tennis, driven largely by José's obsessive coaching, became a double-edged sword. Success in tennis was both a source of pride and a reminder of the pressures that dominated his life. By his late teens, Erik began to withdraw, feeling increasingly isolated under the weight of expectations that felt more like a prison than a path to personal fulfillment.

Unable to openly defy his father, Erik's rebellion manifested in subtler ways. He grew more anxious, more uncertain, and in his search for an outlet, he too turned to acts of delinquency. In 1988, Erik became involved in a string of burglaries, an act that seemed almost inexplicable for a young man of privilege. The incident shocked José, who saw it as a betrayal, a direct affront to the values he had instilled in his sons. But for Erik, these thefts represented something deeper—a cry for freedom, an attempt to assert control over his own life in the only way he felt he could. Like Lyle, Erik was rebelling against the rigid expectations that had defined his existence, though his actions were veiled in secrecy and guilt, adding yet another layer of tension within the household.

As these cracks in the family's facade grew, so did the divide between the brothers and their parents. José, rather than recognizing his sons' struggles as signs of distress, saw their actions as failures, as threats to the integrity of the family's image. His response was to clamp down harder, to intensify his control, believing that more discipline would set his sons back on the "right" path. Kitty, trapped in her own battles with depression and alcoholism, was unable to offer the boys the guidance and support they so desperately needed. Her presence in their lives was one of inconsistency, a mother who loved her children but was often too consumed by her own pain to intervene in meaningful ways.

The strain on the family continued to build, creating an environment where love felt conditional and achievements were the only currency of worth. The harder José pushed, the more both boys felt compelled to resist, leading to an escalating cycle of rebellion and repression. At its core, the Menendez family dynamic was a tug-of-war between appearance and reality, between a father's vision of perfection and the sons who were drowning under the pressure to live up to it.

What the world saw was a successful family—wealthy, respected, and tightly knit. But within the walls of their Beverly Hills mansion, the Menendez household was spiraling into dysfunction. Lyle and Erik's rebellion was more than teenage defiance; it was a symptom of a deeper, more insidious breakdown in the family structure. They were beginning to understand that they would never truly be allowed to carve their own identities, that their lives would forever be measured by standards they hadn't chosen and could never fully satisfy.

In time, these signs of strain and rebellion would become more than just quiet acts of defiance. They would lay the groundwork for a tragedy that no one, not even José with his unyielding grip on control, could prevent. The Menendez brothers were slipping through the cracks, each act of rebellion a step closer to a breaking point from which there would be no return. The stage was being set, quietly and inexorably, for a family implosion that would shock the world and reveal, in painful detail, the true cost of a life lived in pursuit of a distorted vision of perfection.

Part II:

THE DARK SECRETS

Chapter Three

Allegations of Abuse and Family Trauma

Accusations of Sexual and Emotional Abuse

As the investigation into the Menendez murders deepened, a chilling narrative began to emerge, casting the family's past in a harsh, unforgiving light. Beneath the polished image of a successful, affluent family lay stories of trauma and secrets that had remained hidden for years, only coming to light in the most tragic and public way. In the courtrooms that would soon be filled with lawyers, journalists, and spectators, the Menendez brothers, Lyle and Erik, would make allegations that would shock the nation: they had not simply been the rebellious sons of a domineering father; they were survivors of a family life marred by sexual and emotional abuse.

The accusations did not fit with the image the public had of the Menendez family. To most, José Menendez was a formidable figure—an immigrant success story who had built a powerful career in the entertainment industry, a man who demanded excellence not just from himself but from everyone around him. But to Lyle and Erik, he was something else entirely. Behind closed doors, the man they called "Father" was, according to their testimony, a figure of fear and control, a man who used not only his words but his physical presence to instill obedience. They would later describe a life in which love was intertwined with terror, where the very person they looked up to was also the one who caused them profound harm.

In the hushed tones of their courtroom testimonies, Lyle and Erik recounted memories that were both horrifying and heartbreaking. They claimed that José's abuse began when they were young children, blurring the lines between discipline and domination, affection and exploitation. For years, they had allegedly endured repeated sexual abuse at the hands of their father, abuse that they felt was supported, or at least ignored, by their mother, Kitty. According to the brothers, Kitty had been aware of José's actions but had either been too powerless or too broken to intervene. This revelation painted a tragic portrait of Kitty as a mother who was trapped within her own pain and denial, a woman unable or unwilling to protect her children from the nightmare unfolding within their home. The allegations of abuse cast a new, haunting perspective on the brothers' lives and the pressures they faced growing up. José, who was already seen as a controlling figure, was now accused of using his power in the most intimate and destructive way possible. The courtroom heard disturbing details about how the abuse had allegedly shaped Lyle and Erik's lives, how it had affected their ability to trust, and how it had led them to develop complex psychological scars that they carried into adulthood. For them, the mansion in Beverly Hills had not been a haven of security and privilege; it had been a prison, a place where they were held captive not only by the demands of their father's ambitions but by the daily trauma they endured in silence. The courtroom became a theater of pain, with Lyle and Erik recounting moments that no child should ever experience. They spoke of a father who used his authority and influence to silence them, to force them into submission, and to strip them of the innocence that should have defined their childhood. Each accusation peeled back another layer of the Menendez family's pristine facade, exposing a family dynamic rooted in fear rather than love, manipulation rather than guidance. For many, it was difficult to reconcile these allegations with the image of José as a successful executive, a man respected by his colleagues and revered for his achievements. Yet, as the brothers continued to share their memories, the image of the Menendez household grew darker and more complex, revealing the anguish and horror that they claimed lay beneath the surface.

The abuse was not just physical; it was deeply emotional, affecting every aspect of the brothers' lives. José's dominance was pervasive, affecting how they saw themselves, how they interacted with others, and how they coped with the expectations placed upon them. Lyle described how his father would belittle and demean him, using harsh words to erode his sense of self-worth, to ensure that his sons remained in a constant state of submission. Erik, quieter and more introspective, suffered in silence, internalizing the trauma that left him feeling isolated and unworthy. The brothers claimed that José used psychological manipulation to control them, shaping their thoughts, emotions, and behaviors to fit his vision, leaving them with little sense of autonomy or self-respect. The accusations of abuse sent shockwaves through the courtroom and the nation. In a society that was just beginning to grapple with the realities of child abuse and its long-term effects, the Menendez case forced the public to confront uncomfortable questions. How could such horrifying actions go unnoticed within a family that seemed so outwardly successful? Was it possible that the pursuit of status and success had blinded Kitty and others close to the family to the pain that was festering within? And perhaps most hauntingly, could the brothers' alleged suffering have driven them to commit the unthinkable?

As the details of the alleged abuse unfolded, public opinion began to waver. The image of the Menendez brothers as cold-blooded killers, driven by greed, started to blur, replaced by a more complex, tragic picture of young men shaped by trauma and pain. The defense argued that Lyle and Erik had reached a breaking point, that the years of abuse and manipulation had left them feeling as though violence was their only escape. The testimonies of sexual and emotional abuse were not just attempts to mitigate their guilt; they were pleas for understanding, explanations for why two sons might feel they had no choice but to turn against their parents.

In recounting these painful memories, Lyle and Erik sought to reveal the hidden darkness of their lives, to shed light on the invisible scars that had shaped them. For some, these allegations evoked sympathy, a sense of tragedy that underscored the fragility of human life and the consequences of unchecked power within a family. For others, the testimonies raised doubts, suspicions that the brothers were using their claims as a defense tactic, a way to justify the brutal act they had committed.

But regardless of how their words were interpreted, one thing was clear: the Menendez family was not what it seemed. Behind the walls of their luxurious home, beyond the trappings of wealth and success, lay a history of pain that could no longer be ignored. The allegations of abuse were more than a twist in a legal case; they were a window into the psychological and emotional devastation that, according to the brothers, defined their lives. And as these revelations spilled out in court, they painted a picture of a family where love had been overshadowed by control, where protection had been replaced by exploitation, and where the American Dream had been warped into a nightmare that no one saw coming.

Impact on the Brothers' Mental Health

The impact of the alleged abuse on Lyle and Erik Menendez went far beyond the immediate fear and pain they described in court. It seeped into the deepest parts of their psyche, shaping the young men they became, casting long shadows over their perceptions of self-worth, trust, and security. By the time they stood trial, the brothers were not only bearing the weight of their parents' brutal deaths but also the profound psychological scars left by years of manipulation, fear, and trauma. The mental health impact was evident not only in their actions but in their demeanor and testimonies—haunted, hesitant, and broken in ways that were sometimes visible only to those who looked closely.

For Lyle, the abuse had fostered a complex mix of defiance and guilt, an internal battle between the desire to rebel against his father's control and the guilt of feeling as though he could never live up to the impossible standards set for him. From a young age, Lyle learned that love and approval were conditional, something that had to be earned through achievement and obedience. José's constant criticism and exacting demands chipped away at his self-confidence, leaving him with a nagging sense of inadequacy. Despite his outward bravado, Lyle's confidence was fragile, his sense of self-worth dependent on meeting his father's expectations. Yet, the more he tried, the more he failed to find acceptance, and the resulting internal conflict began to fuel his resentment and, eventually, his anger.

This toxic cycle of striving for approval and facing rejection led Lyle down a path of rebellion cloaked in privilege. His actions—cheating in school, dabbling in petty crimes—were cries for autonomy, small acts of resistance against the man who controlled every aspect of his life. But these acts only deepened his self-loathing, as each attempt to assert his independence was met with José's swift and unyielding punishment. Over time, the abuse blurred the lines between love and resentment, filling Lyle with an overwhelming mix of emotions he couldn't fully comprehend or express. His mental health was marked by internalized rage and self-blame, a cocktail of unprocessed trauma that left him struggling to reconcile his feelings toward his father and, by extension, toward himself.

Erik's response to the alleged abuse was markedly different but equally devastating. While Lyle leaned into defiance, Erik withdrew into himself, becoming quieter, more introspective, and increasingly anxious. The pressure to meet his father's standards and the trauma of abuse created a profound sense of isolation within him. José's relentless pursuit of control left Erik feeling powerless, robbing him of his own identity and planting seeds of self-doubt that would follow him into adulthood. Unlike Lyle, who sometimes dared to push against the boundaries, Erik internalized his pain, becoming hyper-aware of his father's gaze, hyper-vigilant to the possibility of failure or disapproval.

The abuse didn't just affect Erik's sense of self; it fundamentally altered his ability to trust others. José's betrayal of his role as protector left Erik suspicious and fearful, even in situations where he was safe. His relationships were strained, marked by a deep-rooted mistrust and a lingering sense of unworthiness. He had learned to live in a state of constant fear, watching every word, every move, trying to avoid incurring his father's wrath. This pervasive anxiety became a permanent fixture in his mind, eroding his confidence and leaving him feeling as though he were trapped in an endless cycle of helplessness. As a result, Erik's mental health began to deteriorate, his spirit crushed under the weight of his father's control and his mother's indifference.

In later years, this trauma manifested in both brothers as severe depression and, in Erik's case, suicidal ideation. The psychological toll of living under such intense and traumatic circumstances created a void within them, a profound emptiness that no amount of material wealth could fill. While they may have appeared, on the surface, as privileged young men, their minds bore the invisible scars of their experiences, scars that would shape every decision they made, every relationship they formed, and, ultimately, their violent response to the lives they had been forced to lead.

As the brothers described their mental anguish in court, experts testified about the lasting effects of such abuse on a child's development. Years of trauma had left them with symptoms commonly associated with post-traumatic stress disorder (PTSD)—hyper-vigilance, flashbacks, nightmares, and severe emotional detachment. The intense control their father exercised over their lives had left them unable to see a way out, to envision any future free from the shadow of their trauma. These symptoms painted a picture of two young men whose lives had been shaped not by normal parental guidance but by a pervasive, insidious terror that had taken root in their minds, affecting every corner of their lives.

Their defense argued that the years of abuse and trauma had driven the brothers to a breaking point, a psychological state where they felt trapped and desperate, with no one to turn to and no hope for escape. In the distorted lens of their trauma, the only way to end the suffering seemed to be to eliminate the source. For Lyle and Erik, the alleged abuse did not merely shape their childhood; it redefined their relationship with reality, pushing them into a world where violence felt like the only means of survival.

To the public, the Menendez brothers had once been seen as killers motivated by greed. But with each revelation of their mental anguish, a new understanding began to emerge—a recognition of the profound psychological scars left by years of trauma. The world began to see Lyle and Erik not just as perpetrators, but as victims, haunted by the actions of a father who should have protected them and a mother who could not or would not help. The brothers' mental health struggles were not just background details in a sensational crime; they were central to understanding the depth of suffering that had unfolded behind the closed doors of the Menendez household.

Friends and Family Testimonies: The Other Side of the Story

As Lyle and Erik Menendez laid bare their allegations of abuse in the courtroom, a wave of shock rippled through friends, family, and the public. The narrative they presented was one that drastically conflicted with the image most people had of the Menendez family. Friends and relatives who had known the family, spent time in their Beverly Hills mansion, and shared moments with José and Kitty, were confronted with a story that seemed impossible, unimaginable. How could a family that appeared so successful, so picture-perfect, be hiding such horrific secrets? The testimony from those close to the Menendez family became pivotal, offering alternative perspectives that cast doubt, context, and sometimes even unwitting support to the brothers' claims.

The friends and family members who took the stand provided glimpses into the Menendez household that, at times, both supported and contradicted Lyle and Erik's accounts. Some, especially those closest to José, struggled to believe the accusations. To them, José was a disciplined, driven man, perhaps strict, but never monstrous. Many of his colleagues admired his ambition, his rise from a Cuban immigrant to a powerful entertainment executive, and his relentless pursuit of success. Friends recalled José's pride in his sons, how he would speak of their achievements, especially in sports, and how he wanted nothing more than for them to excel. They acknowledged that he could be demanding, but to them, this was typical of a father who wanted the best for his children.

These testimonies painted José as a father driven by traditional values, a man who saw discipline as essential to raising successful children in a challenging world. Yet, as witnesses shared their stories, certain details began to emerge that subtly hinted at a more complex and darker side of José's personality. Some friends admitted that José was not known for his warmth or patience; he was, in many ways, an authoritarian figure, a man who expected compliance and perfection. This strict demeanor, while understandable to some, appeared harsher when viewed in the context of Lyle and Erik's claims, casting his rigid parenting style in a more troubling light.

Other testimonies came from extended family members who had known José and Kitty from their earlier years. Some expressed disbelief at the allegations, particularly those concerning sexual abuse. For them, the idea that José could have engaged in such behavior was inconceivable. They spoke of José as a disciplined, highly focused individual, almost to the point of being emotionally distant, but never as someone capable of the crimes his sons described. Kitty, too, was portrayed by some family members as a loving, if sometimes fragile, mother who cared deeply for her children. These family members could not reconcile the accusations with the couple they had known, insisting that whatever faults José and Kitty might have had, they did not align with the monstrous portrait painted by Lyle and Erik.

Yet, as the testimonies continued, a few voices stood out, quietly validating the underlying dysfunction in the Menendez household. One of the most notable witnesses was a cousin who had been close to Lyle and Erik during their childhood. She recounted moments where the boys had hinted at troubles at home, where they seemed anxious or fearful in ways that, looking back, seemed abnormal for young children. She recalled a particularly haunting conversation with Lyle, in which he had hinted at "something bad" happening within the family, though he had not provided specifics. This cousin's testimony suggested that the Menendez brothers' claims might not have been fabrications, that there was, indeed, an undercurrent of pain and fear within their seemingly perfect lives.

Moreover, a former friend of Erik's added a troubling layer to the narrative. This friend testified that Erik had once confided in him about being fearful of his father, that he felt constantly on edge and struggled with a sense of helplessness at home. While Erik had never explicitly mentioned abuse, this friend recalled Erik's anxiety, his reluctance to discuss his family life in detail, and his tendency to avoid certain topics. It was clear, he said, that Erik's relationship with his father was fraught with tension, far from the image of a supportive and nurturing household.

One of the most impactful testimonies came from Judalon Smyth, the former lover of Dr. Jerome Oziel, the therapist who had recorded Lyle and Erik's confessions. Smyth, despite her own complicated relationship with Oziel, testified that the brothers had revealed their allegations of abuse during their sessions, recounting memories that were deeply traumatic and specific. Although her credibility was questioned due to her personal issues with Oziel, her account added weight to the brothers' story, especially as she had no apparent motive to support their claims beyond recounting what she had heard.

The testimonies from friends and family members created a dichotomy within the court. On one hand, there were those who saw José and Kitty as misunderstood parents, strict but well-meaning, whose sons had perhaps invented or exaggerated their stories to escape punishment. On the other hand, there were those who had seen cracks in the family's foundation, who believed that, behind the polished image, there had been signs of a deeper dysfunction—a dysfunction that could explain the tragedy that had unfolded.

These testimonies left the courtroom and the public in a state of uncertainty, torn between two opposing realities. The Menendez brothers' defense team argued that the testimonies that hinted at José's harsh parenting style and the boys' unusual behaviors were evidence of the abuse they had endured. The prosecution, however, framed these details as typical of a wealthy, high-achieving family, where discipline and high expectations were sometimes mistaken for cruelty.

In the end, the testimonies from friends and family provided no definitive answers, only fragments of insight into a family marked by contradictions. For every voice that doubted the brothers' allegations, there was another that suggested the possibility of hidden pain, of a family life that was far more complicated than it appeared. The testimonies underscored a tragic reality—that sometimes, the truth of a family's dysfunction is visible only in hindsight, when the pieces no longer fit neatly together, and the pain of the past becomes impossible to ignore.

These conflicting accounts became yet another layer of complexity in the Menendez case. They challenged the simplistic narrative of greedy sons driven by wealth, painting instead a picture of two young men caught in a family structure that, whether through overt abuse or insidious control, had left them broken and desperate. And while the testimonies did not provide the clarity the public or the court sought, they deepened the understanding of the Menendez family's inner life, revealing a story that was as much about trauma and perception as it was about crime.

Chapter Three- *The Descent into Darkness*

Erik's Rebellion: Burglary and Therapy with Dr. Oziel

Erik Menendez's rebellion was quieter, more subdued than that of his older brother, Lyle, but it was no less significant. As a sensitive, introspective young man, Erik had always seemed more vulnerable, his responses shaped by fear rather than defiance. While Lyle's resistance to their father's control often took the form of bold, visible acts of rebellion, Erik's dissent unfolded in shadows, hidden beneath layers of anxiety and guilt. His spirit was one that sought refuge, that internalized his father's disappointment and expectations, struggling to maintain the façade of the obedient son while slowly unraveling inside. By his teenage years, Erik's pain and frustration had become too great to contain, leading him down a dangerous path that he neither fully understood nor could control.

In 1988, Erik's inner turmoil finally spilled into his actions. Desperate for some semblance of control in his life, he found himself drawn into a series of burglaries, a choice that seemed shocking for a young man of privilege but made sense within the context of his stifling home life. To outsiders, the notion of Erik Menendez, the son of a millionaire living in Beverly Hills, resorting to theft was bewildering, almost absurd. Why would someone with every material advantage available to him resort to such a crime? But Erik's decision wasn't about money or possessions; it was about freedom—freedom from the oppressive control of his father, freedom from the gnawing emptiness that had come to define his life. Each burglary was an act of defiance cloaked in secrecy, a dangerous release that temporarily dulled the pain of his reality.

These thefts were more than adolescent mischief. For Erik, they represented a daring attempt to assert his autonomy, to push back against the forces that had shaped him without his consent. In each break-in, he felt a brief, liberating surge, a momentary escape from the rigid expectations that governed every aspect of his existence.

It was a rebellion that spoke of deep-seated anger and frustration, a cry for help wrapped in the thrill of risk. And yet, as exhilarating as these moments were, they were fleeting. When the high wore off, he was left with a stronger sense of guilt, the dread of being caught, and the weight of his father's judgment—if he ever found out.

It didn't take long for Erik's actions to catch up with him. When he was eventually apprehended, the consequences could have been dire. José, a man whose life was built on his reputation, would have been devastated to learn that his son—a Menendez, a boy raised in the luxury of Beverly Hills—had been involved in such an act. But somehow, José managed to keep the incident hidden from public view, arranging for Erik to avoid jail time through a court-ordered therapy arrangement. In a sense, José's intervention reinforced the patterns of control that had governed Erik's life since childhood. Even in his rebellion, Erik found himself shielded and silenced, his actions managed to avoid tarnishing the Menendez family's perfect image.

Erik was sent to therapy with Dr. Jerome Oziel, a psychologist known for his unconventional methods and complex personality. The sessions with Dr. Oziel were meant to help Erik confront his underlying issues, a chance to understand the roots of his actions and perhaps find a path back to stability. However, the therapy sessions soon took on a life of their own, evolving into something far more intimate and fraught than standard psychological treatment. Dr. Oziel quickly became aware that Erik's problems went deeper than teenage rebellion. Beneath Erik's soft-spoken demeanor and nervous energy lay years of unresolved pain and trauma, experiences that Erik had buried so deeply he could barely articulate them.

In the sterile setting of Dr. Oziel's office, Erik began to open up, cautiously revealing fragments of his strained relationship with his father and his struggle to cope with the overwhelming pressures he faced at home. There, in those sessions, he touched on the complex blend of fear and resentment he felt toward José, a father he both idolized and dreaded. Dr. Oziel sensed that Erik's rebellious actions were symptoms of a far darker reality than a privileged teenager's dalliance with delinquency. Erik's descriptions of life under his father's rule were tinged with an unmistakable sorrow, as though he were trapped in a life he could neither embrace nor escape.

Yet, even with Dr. Oziel, Erik's disclosures were limited, guarded by years of conditioning that had taught him never to question, never to speak out against his family. He would reveal small details, only to retract them, his fear evident in the way he spoke of his father and his family life. Dr. Oziel, sensing the depth of Erik's turmoil, encouraged him to delve deeper, to unearth the memories and feelings that had driven him to such desperate acts. The sessions became an exploration of Erik's fractured psyche, each revelation peeling back layers of repression and pain that had been carefully hidden.

For Erik, these therapy sessions offered a space where he could glimpse the possibility of being seen, of having his voice heard. But they also became a dangerous dance between vulnerability and fear, a tightrope walk where he risked exposing the secrets he had spent years trying to forget. Dr. Oziel, aware of the sensitivity of Erik's admissions, began to see the full extent of the dysfunction within the Menendez family. What had initially appeared as a case of teenage rebellion was now emerging as a narrative steeped in trauma, a cry for help that went beyond mere behavioral correction.

These sessions would eventually become the foundation of the case against the brothers, as Erik, in a moment of vulnerability, disclosed the family's deepest, darkest secrets, bringing to light the allegations of abuse that would later shake the nation. But in those early days of therapy, before the case became a media spectacle, Erik's sessions with Dr. Oziel were less about confession and more about survival—a tentative attempt to untangle himself from the chains of his past, even if he didn't yet know how.

Ultimately, Erik's descent into burglary and his time with Dr. Oziel marked a turning point in his life, a period where the fractures in his mind began to show, where the weight of his family's hidden dysfunction started to surface in dangerous and visible ways. For the young man who had grown up suppressing his pain, these acts of rebellion and these moments in therapy were the beginning of a journey that would lead to an explosive release of all the emotions he had kept buried. In trying to break free from his father's grip, Erik was setting into motion a path that would ultimately lead both him and his brother to a place from which they could never return.

Lyle's Struggles at Princeton

Lyle Menendez arrived at Princeton University with all the advantages and expectations that came with being José Menendez's eldest son. Princeton was a carefully chosen destination, selected not just for its prestige but for what it represented: another milestone in José's meticulously planned vision for Lyle's life. For José, Princeton wasn't just a university; it was a proving ground, a place where Lyle was expected to forge the connections and build the academic foundation that would cement his future in the family legacy. But for Lyle, stepping into Princeton's ivy-covered walls was less about fulfilling dreams and more about the relentless burden of his father's ambitions.

From the beginning, Lyle's experience at Princeton was fraught with tension and pressure. While he wore the title of "Princeton student" like a badge of honor, the reality of his life there was far from the collegiate ideal. He carried with him the weight of his father's expectations, a pressure that suffocated any sense of personal aspiration. Lyle wasn't there to discover his own path; he was there to fulfill a role predetermined by his father, a role that required nothing less than perfection. And, in the isolation of this elite institution, where he was surrounded by peers who seemed genuinely invested in their futures, Lyle felt increasingly like an imposter, going through the motions of a life that was never truly his own.

Academically, Lyle struggled to keep up. The demands of Princeton's rigorous coursework collided with his lingering sense of inadequacy, a feeling that had been drilled into him through years of his father's relentless critique. To José, Lyle was never quite enough—each achievement was met with either muted approval or thinly veiled disappointment, a cycle that left Lyle perpetually striving but never truly succeeding in his own eyes. This struggle became particularly acute at Princeton, where he quickly realized that his peers were not only brilliant but often more passionate and focused. Unlike them, Lyle was navigating his coursework not out of a desire for learning but out of fear of disappointing his father. This difference left him feeling disconnected, unmotivated, and ultimately, directionless.

In his attempt to keep up, Lyle began cutting corners, desperate to meet the standards expected of him but unable to muster the drive to excel in a field he hadn't chosen for himself. The pressure mounted with each passing semester until, in a moment of desperation, he made a decision that would alter his future irrevocably: he plagiarized an assignment. For Lyle, this act was a quiet rebellion, a slip that reflected the deeper fractures in his psyche. It was as if he were silently declaring, "I can't do this anymore," though he lacked the words to say it out loud. The plagiarism was discovered, and Lyle was promptly suspended, a consequence that, for any student, would have been devastating. But for Lyle, it was more than a punishment—it was a catastrophic blow to his self-worth, a confirmation of the deep-seated belief that he could never measure up.

The suspension was a moment of reckoning, both for Lyle and for his relationship with José. News of the incident sent his father into a spiral of anger and disappointment. For José, the suspension wasn't just Lyle's failure; it was a reflection on him, a stain on the perfect image he had worked so hard to build. José's reaction was swift and unforgiving. He confronted Lyle with a barrage of criticism and shame, underscoring every hurtful word with the implication that Lyle had squandered not only his own potential but also the sacrifices José had made to give him this opportunity.

Lyle, already struggling with feelings of inadequacy, internalized his father's fury, allowing it to deepen the fractures within him. The suspension became symbolic of his perceived worthlessness, a failure that he believed would forever define him in his father's eyes. Any hint of support or understanding from José was absent; instead, he saw only disappointment and anger, emotions that reinforced the belief that he was fundamentally flawed, incapable of living up to the impossible standards set for him.

Back in the family's orbit, away from the intellectual freedom and social opportunities that Princeton had promised, Lyle sank into a quiet despair. His suspension left him with an unsettling realization: his life was not his own. The aspirations he'd been pursuing, the goals he'd worked towards, were never truly his—they were José's, reflections of a dream Lyle was expected to embody. In losing his place at Princeton, he had, in some ways, also lost his sense of self. The realization was both painful and disorienting, yet it lacked the freedom that self-discovery typically brings. Instead, Lyle found himself trapped in a cycle of guilt and shame, his future now a blank slate but not one he felt empowered to fill.

The events at Princeton marked a turning point for Lyle, deepening the quiet rebellion that had been growing inside him for years. His suspension served as an unofficial initiation into a world where failure was not only possible but, for the first time, something he allowed himself to confront. Away from the structured, success-driven path José had set for him, Lyle began to explore his limits—not in the healthy sense of self-discovery, but through acts that chipped away at his father's control.

For Lyle, the suspension had exposed the fragility of the life José had built for him, illuminating the shallow foundation upon which his future was meant to stand. It was a rebellion without a clear direction, a simmering resentment that didn't yet have an outlet but was gaining momentum with each passing day. Lyle's struggle at Princeton, and the suspension that followed, was the beginning of a deeper descent, a path that would eventually lead him away from his father's expectations and toward choices that would alter the trajectory of his life forever. In the quiet aftermath of his failure, Lyle began to see the cracks in the narrative his father had crafted for him, and though he was still bound by that vision, the seeds of defiance had already been planted, waiting for the moment they would take root and grow into something darker and more definitive.

Confessions and Secrets Revealed in Therapy

Following his suspension from Princeton and the series of missteps that had increasingly distanced him from his father's ideals, Lyle Menendez found himself at a crossroads. The weight of his failures, both real and perceived, had become a haunting burden, and his rebellion—subtle as it had been—had given him little solace. Beneath his outward attempts to appear strong and composed, he was wrestling with a storm of guilt, anger, and a longing for a release from the suffocating expectations that defined his life. It was at this juncture that Lyle joined his brother Erik in sessions with Dr. Jerome Oziel, a therapist who would become both witness and confidant to the unraveling of the Menendez brothers' most guarded secrets.

Initially, the therapy sessions with Dr. Oziel seemed to be an attempt to restore order, to address the behavioral issues that had disrupted their family's pristine image. For José, therapy was a last resort—a chance to bring his sons back in line without public scandal, a way to quietly "fix" them so they could resume the roles he had so carefully planned. But for Lyle and Erik, these sessions became something else entirely. Dr. Oziel's office, a quiet, neutral space far from the control and judgment they endured at home, offered a rare opportunity to speak freely. And, over time, the brothers began to peel back the layers of their guarded lives, each revelation bringing them closer to a terrifying truth they had long buried.

Lyle was the first to break through the wall of silence, his voice hesitant but heavy with years of unspoken pain. As he shared fragments of his life, he began to describe the suffocating control exerted by his father, the constant sense of inadequacy that shadowed him, and the fear that had shaped his every move. He spoke of José's impossible expectations, his explosive temper, and his unyielding standards. But it wasn't until he hinted at a deeper, darker aspect of his upbringing that Dr. Oziel sensed there was more beneath the surface. Lyle struggled to find the words, his voice faltering as he edged closer to the memories he had locked away, memories that were as painful as they were terrifying.

Over the course of several sessions, Lyle began to reveal details that painted a far darker portrait of his relationship with José than anyone had previously imagined. He alluded to instances of emotional and psychological abuse, moments where José's control extended beyond the usual bounds of parental discipline into something far more insidious. With each admission, Lyle's resolve seemed to weaken, as though the memories were too heavy to carry any longer. Eventually, he found himself confessing to something he had spent years trying to forget: allegations of sexual abuse, acts that he claimed had left scars no amount of success or approval could ever heal.

The weight of Lyle's confession stunned Dr. Oziel. Here was a young man, privileged by every outward measure, revealing a hidden life defined by fear and violation. Lyle's story was one of quiet suffering, of a childhood where trust and safety had been twisted into tools of control. The therapist sensed the profound impact these experiences had on Lyle's psyche, how they had shaped his identity, his self-worth, and his relationship with his family. And, as Lyle unburdened himself, the focus of their therapy shifted from correcting behavior to understanding trauma, delving into the root causes of the anger and resentment that had been festering for years.

Yet, even as Lyle began to open up, there remained an unspoken understanding between him and Erik, a silent bond rooted in shared suffering. Erik, who had always been more vulnerable, more anxious, seemed even more hesitant to speak of the past, as though the memories he held were too painful to voice. It was in one of these sessions that Lyle, sensing his brother's hesitation, encouraged Erik to share his own story, to reveal the secrets they had both carried in silence. With Lyle's support, Erik finally broke down, his voice trembling as he recounted his own experiences of alleged abuse at the hands of their father.

Erik's confession was raw and heart-wrenching, his words filled with the anguish of someone who had been forced to hide his pain for most of his life. He described moments of terror, of feeling trapped and powerless under José's control, his life shaped by a constant, lingering dread. The abuse, Erik claimed, had begun when he was very young, evolving from harsh discipline to something far darker. His voice shook as he detailed the ways in which he had been manipulated, how José's presence had loomed over every aspect of his life, erasing any sense of personal agency. Erik spoke of the nightmares that still haunted him, the anxiety that had grown into a constant companion, and the deep-seated shame that left him questioning his worth.

As the brothers shared their confessions with Dr. Oziel, the depth of their trauma became painfully clear. These were not mere grievances against a strict father but the revelations of two young men who had endured years of psychological and physical torment. The therapy sessions were both a release and a reckoning, a chance for Lyle and Erik to confront the ghosts of their past, to give voice to the pain they had buried beneath layers of silence and shame. In these sessions, they found a fleeting sense of validation, a recognition of the suffering they had endured, even if it could never fully erase the impact of those experiences.

Dr. Oziel, caught between his role as therapist and confidant, realized the gravity of what he had heard. These confessions were not just stories; they were cries for help, revelations that spoke to the profound dysfunction hidden within the Menendez family. And as the brothers continued to open up, a picture emerged of a household governed by fear and control, a family structure that had eroded any sense of safety or love. Lyle and Erik were not simply acting out or rebelling; they were coping with years of unaddressed trauma, struggling to reconcile their loyalty to their family with the pain inflicted upon them.

These sessions would, in time, become pivotal in the legal case that followed, with Dr. Oziel's notes and tapes providing a haunting record of the brothers' confessions. But in those initial moments, before the glare of the media and the scrutiny of the court, the therapy room was a place of fragile honesty, a sanctuary where Lyle and Erik could finally speak their truth. Their confessions, though painful, were a step toward understanding themselves and the choices they would soon make, choices that would alter their lives forever.

In that room, amidst the quiet of Dr. Oziel's office, Lyle and Erik Menendez confronted the darkest parts of their past, unveiling secrets that had remained hidden for too long. And as those secrets came to light, they faced an unsettling realization: the life they had known was built on a foundation of fear, a foundation that could no longer support the weight of their trauma. The confessions were a descent into darkness, an acknowledgment of the damage done, and a prelude to the storm that was yet to come. In speaking the truth, they had unlocked something within themselves, something that could no longer be contained.

Part III:

The Murders

Chapter Five - The Night of the Crime

Detailed Account of the August 20, 1989 Murders

The night of August 20, 1989, was a warm Sunday in Beverly Hills, the kind of tranquil evening that masked the darkness about to descend within one of its most exclusive neighborhoods. Inside the lavish Menendez mansion, José and Kitty Menendez settled in for what they expected to be an ordinary night. They had just returned home from a weekend of tennis matches and social events, small but comforting reminders of their privileged, well-curated lives. It was supposed to be a quiet evening, a pause from the demands of José's high-powered career and Kitty's complex struggles with her own personal demons. But that night, the calm of their opulent home would be shattered by an act of violence so brutal that it would send shockwaves across the nation and leave their family legacy in ruins.

The exact details of what unfolded that night remain clouded by the confusion and horror of the events, but the facts, pieced together later from testimonies and forensic evidence, paint a grim picture. Around 10:00 p.m., José and Kitty settled in the family room, unwinding from the day in front of the television. Kitty reclined on the couch, her head resting on a pillow, while José sat nearby, focused on the TV. The house, dimly lit and quiet, seemed to envelop them in a false sense of security. They were, after all, in Beverly Hills—a place where violent crime seemed like an almost foreign concept, something that happened in other parts of Los Angeles, far removed from the manicured lawns and guarded estates of Elm Drive.

Unknown to José and Kitty, Lyle and Erik were about to enter the room, each armed with a 12-gauge shotgun. The brothers had spent hours contemplating their decision, but in those moments leading up to the act, the line between fear, anger, and desperation blurred into a haze. In their minds, they had convinced themselves that this was the only way to free themselves from the grip of a lifetime of trauma and control, a haunting past that they believed they could escape only through this irreversible act. But whatever justifications or explanations filled their minds in those tense moments, the reality of what they were about to do would forever stain the walls of the home they had once sought sanctuary in.

Without warning, Lyle and Erik entered the family room, their presence casting long shadows over their unsuspecting parents. In a split second, they raised their guns, and the silence was ripped apart by the thunderous sound of the first shotgun blast. The shot struck José, who slumped forward in his chair, his body thrown into a state of shock and sudden paralysis. He likely didn't even have a chance to register what was happening before the next shot rang out. Kitty, startled awake, looked around in terror, disoriented by the sudden eruption of violence and the sight of her husband lying bloodied and motionless. Her initial shock quickly morphed into sheer panic as she realized that her own sons were the source of the horror unfolding before her.

In a frenzy of terror, Kitty attempted to scramble away, but her movements were hampered by the shock and confusion that left her paralyzed with fear. She tried to make sense of the unimaginable reality: her own children, standing before her, guns pointed, their faces hardened with a resolve that was chilling and unreadable. As she attempted to shield herself, the next rounds were fired, bullets tearing through her body, ending any chance of escape. The initial shots wounded her, but the assault continued with relentless precision. Each blast was a brutal punctuation, a horrific final act that left no room for mercy or reprieve. In a matter of moments, Kitty and José Menendez were dead, their lives extinguished by the very people they had brought into the world.

The family room, once a place of routine and comfort, was transformed into a scene of unspeakable violence. The luxury furnishings and tasteful decor were splattered with blood, fragments of a shattered family portrait that now lay in ruin. The house, which had once been a symbol of the Menendez family's success and José's ambition, had become the site of a tragedy so profound it would become etched into the nation's collective memory.

In the immediate aftermath, Lyle and Erik stood in the silence that followed, the echoes of gunfire lingering in the air, mingling with the acrid scent of gunpowder. It was a silence filled with the weight of finality, the realization that they had crossed a boundary from which there would be no return. The brothers, visibly shaken and in shock, tried to compose themselves as they processed the magnitude of what they had just done. What had begun as a night of anticipated liberation had ended in an irrevocable loss of innocence and humanity, leaving them not only parentless but bound to an act they could never undo.

Lyle, the older of the two, attempted to take control of the situation. He suggested that they fabricate an alibi, and the two quickly agreed to stage a scenario that would divert suspicion. Leaving the house, they drove off into the night, heading to a nearby movie theater. There, they purchased tickets to the James Bond film *Licence to Kill*, a macabre irony given what had just transpired. They stayed long enough to create an alibi before returning to their now silent, blood-stained home. Upon discovering the bodies—an act of staged horror—they dialed 911, their voices frantic with what sounded like genuine anguish.

The recording of the 911 call would later become infamous, with Erik's voice breaking as he cried, "Someone killed my parents!" To the dispatcher, it sounded like raw grief, but to investigators, the call soon appeared rehearsed, the agony exaggerated. When police arrived at the scene, they found Lyle and Erik in a state of visible distress, their faces streaked with tears as they recounted the "discovery" of their parents' bodies. The brothers described an apparent "mob hit" theory, suggesting that their father's business dealings may have made him a target. Initially, the police seemed to buy into the theory, distracted by the gruesome scene and the tragic image of two young men seemingly devastated by the loss of their parents.

The staged grief and the subsequent alibi held for a time, allowing Lyle and Erik to present themselves to the public as victims of a horrible crime. In the days that followed, they became the focal point of sympathy, two young men grappling with an unfathomable tragedy. Yet, beneath the surface, cracks in their facade began to show. The brothers' grief, once overwhelming, appeared to shift as they began to indulge in the very wealth and privilege that had shaped their lives. In the months following the murders, their behavior became increasingly erratic and suspicious, as they spent lavishly and sought out new experiences with a freedom they had never previously enjoyed.

But on the night of August 20, they were not yet in the spotlight. They were two sons, standing in the ruins of their own making, burdened by a crime they would have to carry for the rest of their lives. As the truth of that night would later unfold, the chilling details of the murder would serve as a grim reminder of the darkness that can lie beneath even the most privileged of lives, and of the depths to which the human mind can sink when pushed beyond its breaking point. In the quiet of that August evening, the Menendez family's story—marked by success, control, and unimaginable tragedy—had reached its brutal conclusion, forever altering the lives of two young men who, in an attempt to escape their past, had sealed their fate in a single, horrifying night.

The Brothers' Initial Alibi and 911 Call

In the immediate aftermath of the murders, Lyle and Erik Menendez found themselves standing in the eerie silence of their family's mansion, their parents' lifeless bodies sprawled amid the shattered remnants of their lives. The echo of gunshots had faded, replaced by the stillness of finality. But as reality settled in, the brothers realized they had to act quickly to cover their tracks, to create an alibi that would keep them clear of suspicion. What followed was a calculated decision that blended shock, adrenaline, and the cold logic of self-preservation—a decision that would be crucial in the hours following the crime.

Lyle, the older brother and, in many ways, the more composed of the two, took charge. They needed to create a story, a scenario that would establish their innocence. They agreed to leave the house, to establish their presence somewhere else, so they couldn't be tied to the murders when they were discovered. Grabbing their car keys, they left the gruesome scene behind and drove into the night, a sense of unreality permeating every moment as they made their way to a nearby movie theater. There, they purchased tickets to the James Bond film *Licence to Kill*, ensuring they were seen in a public space, a place bustling with witnesses who could confirm their alibi if needed.

They didn't stay long. The minutes inside the theater were tense, every second feeling like a countdown to the moment they would need to "discover" the horror back home. The choice of a spy thriller was a bitter irony—two brothers, now playing a role as if they were in a movie themselves, trying to cover their tracks in a real-life act of deception. Once enough time had passed to make their alibi seem believable, they left the theater and returned home, where they would set the stage for the next act in their fabricated story: the discovery of the crime scene and the frantic call to 911.

Upon returning to the mansion, the brothers braced themselves. They entered the house, walking into the family room where the bodies of their parents lay in a nightmarish tableau. Lyle picked up the phone and dialed 911, his voice choked with what sounded like raw, unfiltered horror. "Someone killed my parents!" he cried, his tone panicked, as though the shock of the scene was fresh, the reality only just settling in. Erik's voice soon joined, sobbing uncontrollably, his words almost incoherent as he cried for help. The urgency and fear in their voices would later be analyzed endlessly, their anguish dissected by both the public and experts trying to gauge its authenticity.

The 911 operator on the other end of the line tried to remain calm, asking questions in an attempt to understand the situation. Lyle, sounding desperate, repeated again and again that someone had broken in, that his parents were dead. The hysteria in his tone seemed real, convincing enough to sway the operator's perception of the call as a legitimate plea from a devastated son. Erik, whose emotional response was even more intense, was heard sobbing uncontrollably in the background. For the listeners, it sounded like genuine grief, the heartbreaking sounds of two young men who had just discovered the unimaginable.

Within minutes, police arrived at the scene, greeted by Lyle and Erik, who were visibly distraught. Their faces were streaked with tears, their expressions those of two sons reeling from a profound and sudden tragedy. They repeated their story to the officers, clinging to the theory that it must have been a "mob hit" due to José's business dealings—a narrative they had crafted to explain away the brutality of the crime. They described their father as a powerful man, hinting that he may have made enemies in his line of work, and painted a picture of their parents as innocent victims in a targeted attack. The police, confronted with the horrific scene, initially had little reason to question the brothers' version of events. The devastation was so overwhelming, the image of two young men grieving for their parents so potent, that investigators were inclined to accept the theory at face value.

The alibi and the 911 call were convincing enough to protect the brothers from suspicion in the early stages of the investigation. Friends and family members who heard about the tragedy were filled with sympathy for Lyle and Erik, rallying around them in support. The public, too, saw them as victims—young men whose lives had been torn apart in a single, unimaginable night. The initial shock of the murders had captured the nation's attention, and for a brief moment, the Menendez brothers were perceived not as suspects, but as the heartbroken sons of a powerful man whose influence had, perhaps, led to his own downfall.

But the alibi and 911 call, carefully crafted though they were, began to show cracks over time. Police initially focused on the possibility of a professional hit, but inconsistencies in the brothers' behavior began to emerge. Their grief, genuine as it had seemed in the moments of the 911 call, began to appear less authentic as they started spending freely, indulging in luxuries with the wealth they inherited. What initially looked like the actions of grieving sons started to resemble those of opportunists, casting doubt on the authenticity of their reactions on that fateful night.

As investigators delved deeper, suspicions grew. The story the brothers told, combined with the evidence at the scene, began to unravel under scrutiny. Detectives noted that, contrary to what would be expected in a mob hit, there were no signs of forced entry, no evidence that an outside intruder had been in the house. The brutality of the crime—the excessive number of gunshots, the close-range nature of the attacks—did not fit the profile of a professional assassination. Instead, it bore the hallmarks of something personal, something driven by anger and desperation rather than cold calculation.

The 911 call, once seen as a heartbreaking moment of raw emotion, became a point of analysis, with experts and investigators poring over every word, every inflection, looking for signs of deception. What once sounded like unfiltered grief began to take on a different tone in the eyes of those who now suspected the brothers. Erik's uncontrollable sobs, Lyle's desperate cries—were they expressions of genuine horror, or rehearsed lines in a twisted performance?

As the investigation continued, the once-solid alibi began to crumble, exposing the carefully orchestrated deception that Lyle and Erik had built around themselves. What had initially shielded them from suspicion now became evidence of their potential guilt, an intricate web of lies that, in its very complexity, hinted at the depth of their involvement. The night of August 20, 1989, which they had tried to mask in falsehoods, became a haunting testament to the lengths they would go to escape the life they could no longer bear.

In the end, the brothers' alibi and 911 call—intended to portray them as innocent victims—would become integral pieces of the story that exposed the dark reality of what had truly happened in the Menendez home. And as the world looked on, the myth of their innocence would begin to shatter, revealing not just the horror of a crime but the tragedy of a family torn apart by secrets, lies, and, ultimately, violence.

Shock and Horror: The Crime Scene and Early Investigation

When the Beverly Hills police arrived at the Menendez mansion on the night of August 20, 1989, they were unprepared for the horror awaiting them. As they entered the family's luxurious home, they were immediately struck by the overwhelming silence—a stillness that was only amplified by the opulence surrounding them. The usual grandeur of the home, with its high ceilings, polished marble floors, and tasteful decor, now felt cold, ominous, and eerily lifeless. This was no ordinary crime scene; the brutality of what had transpired behind those walls would soon unfold in ghastly detail, shocking even the most seasoned officers.

The Menendez family room, usually a place for relaxation and gathering, was now a grotesque tableau of violence and bloodshed. The officers' flashlights illuminated the carnage—José and Kitty Menendez lay motionless, their bodies torn apart by the blast of shotgun fire. José's body was slumped over on the couch, his once commanding presence reduced to a lifeless form, his wounds so severe that his face was nearly unrecognizable. The force of the gunfire had left him in a state beyond identification, a gruesome testament to the close-range, relentless nature of the attack.

Kitty's body, sprawled across the floor, bore its own tragic story. She appeared to have struggled, to have fought the terror that confronted her in her last moments. Her injuries told a chilling tale of desperation and horror, a futile attempt to escape the onslaught. The blood spatter on the walls and furniture, the remnants of shattered glass, and the twisted remains of the couch pillows—all of it painted a picture of the sheer savagery of the crime. This was not a calculated, detached act of violence; it was a massacre, a brutal annihilation of two lives within what should have been the sanctuary of their home.

The investigators, though trained to handle the grotesque and unsettling, could not hide their shock. The crime scene bore no signs of the usual hallmarks of a professional hit or burglary gone wrong. There was no forced entry, no evidence of valuables disturbed, no signs of a typical break-in. Instead, everything appeared as it would on any other evening in the life of a wealthy family in Beverly Hills. The scene was disturbingly intimate, suggesting that whoever had committed the murders had not entered as a stranger. The brutality and close proximity of the gunshots suggested that this was not a distant or detached killing, but rather one fueled by rage, a deep-seated personal grievance.

In the initial hours of the investigation, detectives leaned toward the "mob hit" theory, a suggestion planted by Lyle and Erik in their frantic 911 call. José's career as a high-powered entertainment executive provided a plausible connection to such a scenario. He was known for his ruthless approach in business, for his uncompromising drive, and for the enemies he had likely accumulated over the years. But as detectives moved through the scene, piecing together the evidence, doubts began to surface. This didn't feel like the work of professionals; it felt more personal, more emotional—too chaotic and merciless to align with the clinical efficiency of an organized crime execution.

One of the first oddities investigators noted was the shotgun shells scattered around the bodies. In a professional hit, the killers would have likely collected the shells to avoid leaving any traceable evidence. Here, the shells lay abandoned, a detail that seemed careless, almost reckless. Moreover, the sheer number of shots fired was unusual; the killers had continued shooting long after José and Kitty were incapacitated, a detail that hinted at anger rather than mere business. Each blast had left a mark, turning the family room into a scene of overkill, a relentless assault far beyond what was necessary to end two lives. The repeated shots, the close range, the brutal injuries—they all spoke to a level of personal rage, an emotional involvement that professional killers typically avoided.

Detectives also couldn't ignore the behavior of Lyle and Erik, whose grief, initially convincing, began to show cracks under closer scrutiny. In the hours following the murders, the brothers seemed visibly shaken, their faces pale and drawn as they answered the detectives' questions. But their accounts of the night lacked depth, almost as if they were reciting rehearsed lines rather than recounting the genuine trauma of discovering their parents' bodies. Investigators noted how quickly they leaned into the mob hit theory, emphasizing their father's business dealings as a likely motive for the crime. The brothers' insistence on this angle felt too eager, almost as if they were guiding the investigation away from other possibilities.

In the days following the murders, detectives continued to analyze the scene, reconstructing the sequence of events as best they could. Blood spatter analysis and ballistics reports confirmed the close range of the attacks, with gunpowder residue indicating that the shots were fired at point-blank distance. The trajectory of the bullets, the location of the shells, and the positioning of the bodies all suggested that José and Kitty had been sitting in the family room, unaware of the imminent danger, when the first shots were fired. José had likely been killed instantly, but Kitty had tried to flee, her movements evident in the blood trails leading across the room. This desperate attempt at escape added another layer of tragedy, highlighting the terror that must have gripped her in her final moments.

Meanwhile, the mansion itself became a point of fascination for both law enforcement and the media. It was a palatial home, a testament to José Menendez's success, now transformed into the setting of a brutal double homicide. Reporters flocked to Beverly Hills, their cameras capturing the imposing gates, the manicured lawns, and the grand architecture of the house. To the public, it was a chilling juxtaposition—the grandeur of wealth shadowed by the horror of violence. The nation was captivated by the story, a brutal crime set against the backdrop of privilege and power. Speculation ran wild, with headlines blaring sensational theories about mob involvement, family feuds, and revenge plots.

But as the days turned into weeks, the initial shock and horror began to give way to a growing unease within the investigation. Detectives couldn't ignore the peculiar behavior of Lyle and Erik. Their grief, so raw on the night of the murders, began to take on a different hue as they started spending large sums of money, indulging in a lifestyle that seemed incongruous with their recent tragedy. They bought expensive watches, luxury cars, and threw lavish parties, actions that cast doubt on the image of devastated sons. The conspicuous consumption was more than just poor taste; it hinted at an unsettling detachment from the loss they had supposedly suffered.

The investigation began to pivot as detectives shifted their focus. What if the murders weren't the result of an external vendetta or José's business dealings? What if the motive was far closer to home? As law enforcement started to consider the possibility of the brothers' involvement, they revisited the crime scene with new eyes, analyzing each piece of evidence, each inconsistency in the narrative provided by Lyle and Erik. The brutality, the apparent lack of remorse, the excessiveness of the violence—it all started to align with a profile of killers who knew their victims intimately, who harbored deep-seated resentments that had reached a boiling point.

Slowly, the pieces began to fit together, revealing a portrait of a family imploding from within. The mansion, once a symbol of the Menendez family's success, had become a silent witness to the darkness festering beneath its lavish surface. And as the investigation tightened around Lyle and Erik, the nation watched, horrified and riveted, as the shocking details of the Menendez murders began to unravel, exposing the trauma, the secrets, and the deadly consequences of a life lived under unyielding pressure. The horror of the crime scene was just the beginning of a story that would delve into the very heart of a fractured family and a crime that left a permanent scar on the American psyche.

Chapter 6: The Fallout

Suspicion and Surveillance

In the weeks following the brutal murders of José and Kitty Menendez, the public's initial sympathy for Lyle and Erik began to waver as unsettling details about the brothers' behavior emerged. Their alibi, initially accepted at face value, was now under scrutiny, and detectives had started to pick up on subtle inconsistencies in their statements. The image of two grieving sons, once embraced by the media, now seemed out of sync with their actions. The extravagant spending, the carefree attitude, the seemingly celebratory behavior—it all painted a picture that didn't align with the gravity of the tragedy they had supposedly endured. Slowly but surely, suspicion began to swirl around the Menendez brothers, casting a shadow over their lives that grew darker by the day.

Law enforcement officers, sensing that something was off, decided to take a closer look. At first, the investigation had focused outward, following leads tied to José's powerful position in the entertainment industry. Rumors of business rivals, enemies, and even the possibility of a mob hit had led detectives down a maze of dead ends. But the further they delved into the circumstances surrounding José's life, the more it became apparent that the answers they sought might lie closer to home. A shift occurred, and Lyle and Erik Menendez, once considered victims, became persons of interest.

To understand the truth, detectives needed more than conjecture—they needed proof. And so, they began to quietly watch the brothers, implementing surveillance to monitor their movements and interactions. Detectives followed them to exclusive shops, where the brothers purchased Rolex watches, designer clothes, and even a luxury car. Their behavior, characterized by lavish spending and apparent nonchalance, seemed entirely disconnected from the reality of losing both parents. The financial records showed transactions totaling hundreds of thousands of dollars, revealing a spending spree that began almost immediately after the murders. This carefree indulgence suggested that Lyle and Erik were not only adjusting to their newfound wealth but reveling in it, as if finally freed from a constraint they had long endured.

The surveillance soon extended beyond financial monitoring. Detectives set up observation points, tracking the brothers as they frequented high-end restaurants, drove around Los Angeles in their new cars, and partied at upscale clubs. It was an image that contrasted starkly with the grief-stricken personas they had initially presented to the public. Their movements were carefully documented, each transaction, each social interaction adding to a profile that was less of grieving sons and more of young men reveling in a newfound sense of liberation. Investigators couldn't ignore the pattern that was emerging, one that suggested entitlement and a chilling detachment from the horrific events that had transpired within their home.

As surveillance intensified, detectives also began recording the brothers' conversations, hoping to capture something that might crack the case open. Conversations with friends, acquaintances, and even casual remarks became potential evidence. The Menendez brothers, unaware of the extent to which they were being watched, spoke freely about their newfound wealth, their plans for the future, and their intentions to use their inheritance to build a legacy separate from their father's. In these private moments, they revealed dreams that sounded disturbingly hollow in the context of their parents' recent deaths. To the investigators listening in, the tone of these conversations was unsettling; there was no sorrow, no sense of loss—only the excitement of possibility.

Meanwhile, Erik, the younger and more emotionally fragile of the two, began to show signs of strain. The surveillance captured his moments of solitude, his private attempts to process the weight of what they had done. Unlike Lyle, who appeared almost unaffected, Erik was visibly struggling, often retreating into himself, his demeanor betraying cracks in the façade they were attempting to maintain. Detectives noticed his nervous behavior, the moments where he appeared lost in thought, his face etched with a kind of silent turmoil. He would occasionally disappear into isolated areas, seemingly to gather himself, to steel his resolve. Investigators observed these moments with interest, wondering if Erik's visible guilt might eventually lead him to confess.

As suspicion grew, the brothers began to feel the pressure closing in. Friends who had once been supportive began to keep their distance, wary of the rumors circulating around them. Some had noticed the shift in the brothers' behavior and the ways in which their demeanor seemed incongruent with their tragedy. Lyle and Erik attempted to dismiss the doubts, relying on their initial alibi and the mob hit theory as shields against the mounting scrutiny. But the strain of maintaining the pretense was beginning to show, especially in Erik, whose composure seemed to fray with each passing day.

Detectives ramped up their efforts, coordinating with close acquaintances of the Menendez family, probing for any information that might expose the brothers' true motives. Old family friends, distant relatives, and even former employees of the Menendez household were questioned, each conversation carefully orchestrated to gather insights into the family dynamics. As more information came to light, a clearer picture of the brothers' lives began to emerge—one that suggested long-standing resentment, buried anger, and a history of familial tension that few outsiders had been privy to. Detectives uncovered whispers of José's authoritarian parenting style, Kitty's struggles with depression, and the growing pressure the brothers had faced under their father's watchful, unforgiving eye. Each new detail painted a picture of a household rife with hidden dysfunction, and slowly, investigators began to suspect that this was a family with darker secrets than anyone had realized.

The surveillance provided investigators with a mounting pile of circumstantial evidence, enough to suggest that the brothers had both motive and opportunity. But what they needed was a direct link—a confession, or at the very least, an admission of guilt that could tie Lyle and Erik to the murders definitively. Erik, with his visible guilt and emotional instability, was considered the weak link. Detectives theorized that if anyone would break under pressure, it would be him. In a calculated move, they decided to focus their attention on Erik, seeking ways to increase the pressure on him without arousing his suspicion.

Meanwhile, Lyle remained as composed as ever, projecting an aura of confidence and control that seemed unshakeable. He kept close tabs on his brother, subtly reinforcing their shared narrative and reminding Erik of the importance of sticking to their story. But even Lyle's composure couldn't entirely mask the growing tension between them. The stress of surveillance, the prying eyes, the unspoken fears—all of it began to weigh heavily on their relationship, creating a rift that grew wider as the walls closed in.

As detectives observed the brothers with a hawk-like intensity, they waited for one of them to make a misstep. The public, too, was beginning to turn, their initial sympathy waning as stories of the brothers' post-murder spending and cavalier lifestyle became widely known. The Menendez brothers were no longer seen as victims of a brutal crime; they were now subjects of suspicion, their innocence tainted by their own behavior. News reports speculated about their guilt, and whispers of a possible family feud began to emerge. Each new detail chipped away at the brothers' carefully constructed alibi, the cracks in their story widening under the weight of public scrutiny and relentless surveillance.

In these moments, the Menendez brothers found themselves trapped in a tightening web, every action, every word, monitored and dissected by detectives who were becoming more certain by the day that the true story of the Menendez murders was far darker and more complex than it had initially seemed. They were no longer grieving sons; they were suspects in a case that had captivated a nation. And as the surveillance continued, the brothers began to feel the inevitable approach of a reckoning, one that would reveal the truth they had worked so hard to bury. In the end, it was not just the brutality of the murders that shocked the world, but the revelation that the crime had been committed by the very people who were supposed to be José and Kitty's legacy, their future—now shattered beyond repair.

The Brothers' Lavish Spending and Suspicious Behavior

In the days and weeks following the murders of their parents, Lyle and Erik Menendez wasted no time diving headfirst into a life of unrestrained luxury and excess, a behavior that quickly attracted the attention of friends, family, and, eventually, law enforcement. While initial grief had painted them as tragic figures in a media-fueled narrative of privilege marred by violence, their actions soon started to raise eyebrows. Instead of grieving in private or showing signs of emotional devastation, the brothers appeared to be seizing their newfound wealth with an almost manic urgency, indulging in a spree that seemed to signal liberation rather than loss. To the public, their actions began to look less like coping mechanisms and more like the telltale signs of guilt—or, at the very least, indifference.

The Menendez estate, now devoid of its original guardians, had left the brothers with access to millions. José's success in the entertainment industry had amassed a fortune, a legacy that now fell into Lyle and Erik's hands. With substantial life insurance payouts and access to their father's accounts, the brothers suddenly found themselves in control of a financial empire they had been waiting to inherit. But rather than managing it conservatively, they seemed intent on burning through it with reckless abandon.

Lyle, the older and more assertive of the two, led the way, his purchases displaying both a hunger for status and an eagerness to shed any remnants of his father's control. Within days of the murders, he bought a Rolex—a gleaming, unmistakable symbol of wealth that he seemed to wear as a badge of his new freedom. But the spending didn't stop there. Lyle quickly followed up this purchase with a Porsche, a car that matched his newfound image of power and privilege. He began dining at the finest restaurants in Beverly Hills, unburdened by the tragedy that was supposed to have shattered his life. Those who saw him observed a young man relishing the life his father's money could provide, as though he were making up for lost time.

Erik, though quieter and more reserved, was no less indulgent. He bought a Jeep Wrangler, a practical yet stylish choice that allowed him a sense of freedom and identity outside of his father's strict expectations. But Erik's spending had its own touch of excess: he hired a personal tennis coach, shelling out tens of thousands of dollars to refine the skills his father had once forced him to master. This choice was telling—it was as if he was reclaiming tennis on his own terms, removing it from José's shadow. Yet the irony was lost on no one; the money he used to finance this pursuit came directly from the father whose control he had long despised.

Together, the brothers' spree extended to high-end boutiques and luxury services, each purchase further solidifying their transformation from grieving sons to conspicuous consumers. They began traveling, taking exotic vacations, reveling in the freedom of movement and choice that had always eluded them under José's rule. For Lyle and Erik, who had lived under a cloud of relentless expectations, this sudden, unrestricted access to wealth felt intoxicating, almost euphoric. They indulged in expensive clothing, threw lavish parties, and surrounded themselves with a new circle of acquaintances drawn to their wealth and the mystique surrounding their story.

But as their spending spiraled out of control, whispers of their behavior began to circulate. Friends who had once shown sympathy began to feel uneasy, sensing an unnatural detachment in the brothers' demeanor. While grief often manifests in unique ways, the brothers' actions felt distinctly different—cold, calculating, and disturbingly joyful. Their apparent lack of restraint, their inability to hold back in the face of such a massive loss, hinted at something darker. It was almost as if the brothers were celebrating rather than mourning, enjoying their new status as two of the wealthiest young men in Los Angeles.

Lyle's actions in particular raised suspicions. Not content with mere luxury purchases, he used his newfound wealth to buy into businesses, making his mark as a young entrepreneur. He purchased a restaurant in Princeton, where he had once studied, his ambitions seeming to grow in tandem with his spending. To those around him, Lyle's new ventures appeared more than just a distraction—they suggested a sense of entitlement, a desire to build an empire of his own, far from the shadow of his father. But as his financial commitments multiplied, so did the scrutiny. Detectives monitoring his behavior noted his seeming disinterest in privacy, his confidence in a lifestyle that barely acknowledged the tragedy that had taken place. Erik's spending, while not as flashy, was no less concerning to those observing the case. His insecurities and vulnerability became more evident as he attempted to keep pace with his brother's extravagant lifestyle. The once shy, introspective Erik was now living a life of excess, one that seemed at odds with his usual personality. But even as he bought cars, traveled, and indulged in luxuries, Erik struggled with guilt, a fact detectives would later use to their advantage. Beneath the veneer of wealth and freedom, Erik's inner turmoil was visible in subtle ways—a restlessness, a lingering sorrow that he could not completely shake, even amid the glitz and glamour.

As the brothers' behavior grew bolder, so did the suspicions surrounding them. The detectives, already keeping tabs on their movements, saw the brothers' spending as evidence of something far more disturbing than grief. The excess, the apparent glee with which they embraced their new lives, felt like the actions of two young men unburdened, free at last from the overbearing influence of their parents. To investigators, this suggested motive—a desire to escape, to claim a life they had long felt denied. Every Rolex, every car, every lavish dinner served as a silent testament to the lengths they were willing to go to sever ties with their past.

Meanwhile, the media began to pick up on the story, shifting the narrative from one of tragedy to one of scandal. News outlets reported on the brothers' lavish spending, their conspicuous consumption drawing as much attention as the murders themselves. Public opinion began to turn, with headlines questioning the integrity of Lyle and Erik's grief. The once-sympathetic lens through which the public had viewed the brothers was now replaced by a more skeptical, even condemning gaze. For the first time, people began to wonder if the Menendez brothers had not only lost their parents but had orchestrated the loss themselves.

The lavish spending spree would ultimately play a crucial role in the investigation. Detectives leveraged the public's suspicions, using the media frenzy to their advantage, hoping to intensify the pressure on Erik, the more emotionally vulnerable of the two. Friends, acquaintances, and even distant relatives who had observed the brothers' behavior were brought in for questioning, asked to recount any peculiar behavior, any remarks that seemed out of place. Each new revelation about the brothers' indulgent lifestyle added to the growing mountain of circumstantial evidence, painting a picture of two young men who saw their parents' deaths as a doorway to the life they had always desired.

In the end, the Menendez brothers' spending spree became a turning point in the case. What had initially seemed like a tragic story of a family destroyed by violence evolved into a twisted tale of greed, entitlement, and betrayal. The signs were now impossible to ignore. And as detectives pieced together the timeline of their lavish purchases, the pattern of entitlement, and their unrestrained behavior, they began to see the true face of the tragedy—a portrait not of victims, but of perpetrators whose thirst for freedom and wealth had driven them to the unthinkable.

The lavish lifestyle the brothers had so eagerly embraced ultimately betrayed them, revealing a darker truth beneath the surface: their actions were not those of mourners, but of men liberated from the constraints of family, ready to revel in a life paid for by the ultimate betrayal. Their spending became the silent confession, a trail of evidence that would lead investigators to the heart of a crime that shook Beverly Hills and left the world asking how two sons could kill to live a life they believed was rightfully theirs.

The Taped Confession: Dr. Oziel and Judalon Smyth's Role

As the investigation into the Menendez murders intensified, detectives grew increasingly frustrated by the lack of direct evidence tying Lyle and Erik Menendez to the brutal crime. Their suspicions were well-founded, bolstered by the brothers' extravagant spending and the unsettling detachment they displayed in the wake of their parents' deaths. Yet, without a confession or an undeniable link, the case remained circumstantial, a tantalizing puzzle missing its crucial pieces. It was during this tense and uncertain phase of the investigation that an unexpected breakthrough arrived—one that would alter the trajectory of the case and reveal a glimpse into the brothers' darkest secrets. The source of this revelation came from Dr. Jerome Oziel, the therapist the Menendez brothers had confided in, and Judalon Smyth, his former lover, who would prove instrumental in exposing the truth.

Dr. Oziel, a Beverly Hills psychologist, had been treating Erik Menendez in the aftermath of the brothers' crime spree and was privy to more information than anyone realized. Erik, younger and more vulnerable than his brother, had been struggling under the weight of his guilt and emotional turmoil. The lavish spending and newfound freedom offered only temporary distractions, and as the weeks passed, Erik began to unravel. Lyle, sensing his brother's weakness, urged him to confide in Dr. Oziel—a calculated move designed to keep Erik's anxiety under control and prevent him from breaking under the weight of suspicion. What neither brother anticipated was the extent to which Dr. Oziel would become embroiled in their story.

During their therapy sessions, Erik had been initially cautious, sharing only fragments of his emotions, revealing the pain and fear that had accumulated over a lifetime spent under his father's authoritarian rule. But as trust developed between Erik and Dr. Oziel, the young man began to open up more fully. Each session peeled back another layer, moving from vague complaints about family pressure to admissions of resentment and unresolved anger. Over time, Erik confessed what he had been struggling to articulate since the night of the murders—an admission that would ultimately lead to one of the most damning pieces of evidence in the case.

Erik broke down during one session, his voice barely above a whisper as he recounted the events of August 20. With tears streaming down his face, he admitted to killing his parents, detailing the plan he and Lyle had devised and the motivations that had driven them to such a horrifying act. It was a moment of vulnerability, a desperate release of the guilt and fear that had haunted him since the crime. Dr. Oziel, listening intently, realized the gravity of what he was hearing. As Erik described the horror of that night, the shock of each gunshot, the cold calculations that led them there, Dr. Oziel understood he was no longer just a therapist—he was now a witness to a confession that could solve one of the most high-profile murder cases in recent history.

Yet, Dr. Oziel found himself in an ethically and legally ambiguous position. Bound by doctor-patient confidentiality, he wrestled with his duty as a psychologist and his responsibility as a citizen. He understood the implications of keeping this information to himself but also knew the risks of breaking confidentiality, not only for his professional career but for his personal safety. The Menendez brothers were volatile, and Dr. Oziel feared what they might do if they discovered he had revealed their secret.

Complicating matters further was Dr. Oziel's relationship with Judalon Smyth, his former lover and patient. Their relationship was fraught, intense, and, by all accounts, toxic—a dynamic marked by manipulation and emotional turbulence. At some point, Dr. Oziel, feeling the need to confide in someone, shared Erik's confession with Judalon. Whether it was a slip of judgment or a calculated decision, Dr. Oziel's disclosure to Judalon would prove to be pivotal. Judalon, intrigued by the sensational nature of the confession and wary of her own unstable relationship with Oziel, became the unlikely catalyst that would bring the truth to light.

Driven by her own complex motives, Judalon decided to act on the information she possessed. She contacted the Beverly Hills police and informed them of Erik's confession, disclosing details about the murders and revealing that the brothers had indeed confessed to Dr. Oziel. At first, the police were skeptical; the information was explosive, but it came from a questionable source. Judalon's background, her troubled relationship with Oziel, and her perceived instability cast doubt on her credibility. Yet, the specificity of the details she provided matched certain aspects of the crime scene—information that would have been difficult for her to fabricate.

Realizing they had to proceed cautiously, detectives began working to obtain the tapes that contained Erik's confessions. These recordings, made by Dr. Oziel during his sessions with the brothers, contained Erik's damning admissions in his own words. However, a legal battle ensued over whether the tapes could be admitted as evidence. The tapes fell into a gray area of confidentiality and privilege, and the defense argued that doctor-patient confidentiality protected them from being used in court. But the stakes were too high, and the prosecution fought tirelessly to gain access to these recordings, aware that they could serve as the linchpin in the case against the Menendez brothers.

Eventually, after months of legal wrangling, the California Supreme Court ruled that two of the tapes could be admitted as evidence. These tapes contained Erik's chilling confessions, recounting the events of that August night with haunting clarity. In the recordings, Erik could be heard detailing the plan he and Lyle had devised, the moments leading up to the murders, and the cold, calculated actions that had turned their parents' lives into ashes. The tapes captured the remorse, the anxiety, and the twisted sense of relief that had washed over him after committing the crime. It was the voice of a young man grappling with unimaginable guilt, yet simultaneously acknowledging the freedom he felt after years of repression and control.

The impact of the tapes was immediate and devastating for the defense. Here was irrefutable proof of the brothers' guilt, Erik's own words sealing their fate in a way that circumstantial evidence never could. For the public, the taped confessions were a shocking revelation, transforming the narrative from a tragic mystery to a tale of betrayal, greed, and a chilling lack of remorse. The audio was raw, unfiltered—a glimpse into the psyche of two young men who had not only killed their parents but had confided the gruesome details in a therapist's office, believing that their secret would remain safe.

Dr. Oziel's role in the case became controversial. While he had ultimately provided critical evidence, his involvement and relationship with Judalon Smyth were called into question. Judalon's motivations, too, were scrutinized, her decision to come forward seen by some as an act of vengeance rather than a pursuit of justice. The ethical boundaries in the case were blurred, with Dr. Oziel and Judalon becoming unlikely players in a legal drama that was as complex and layered as the murders themselves.

Ultimately, the taped confessions became the cornerstone of the prosecution's case. The voices of Erik and Lyle, stripped of pretense and alibi, revealed a level of premeditation and intent that underscored the brutality of their actions. These tapes allowed the court, and the public, to understand the depth of planning that had gone into the murders, the motivations that had driven two sons to commit such a heinous act. The cold detachment, the calculated moves, and the unrepentant tone of the confessions shattered any remaining sympathy for the brothers, reframing them as architects of a crime born not only out of fear but out of a desire for freedom and control. The revelation of the taped confessions was a turning point in the Menendez case, transforming it from a tragic tale of possible misunderstanding to a narrative of calculated betrayal. In those recordings, the brothers were stripped of their facade, their guilt laid bare. And as the tapes played in the courtroom, the truth became undeniable: Lyle and Erik Menendez had orchestrated the brutal end of their parents' lives, and in doing so, had unwittingly set in motion the chain of events that would bring their own world crashing down.

Part IV:

The Trials

Chapter 7: The First Trial

Prosecution vs. Defense: A Battle of Narratives

The first trial of Lyle and Erik Menendez was a courtroom spectacle unlike any other, a complex and emotionally charged clash that would captivate the nation and divide public opinion. It was not just a case about two sons accused of murdering their parents; it was a battle of narratives, a collision of interpretations about what could drive two young men to commit such a horrifying act. On one side stood the prosecution, resolute in their portrayal of the Menendez brothers as cold-blooded killers motivated by greed and entitlement. On the other side was the defense, which painted a starkly different picture—a story of unimaginable abuse and desperation, a tragic culmination of years of hidden suffering and terror. The stakes were life or death, and the courtroom became an arena where every detail, every nuance, was scrutinized in the fight to define the truth.

The prosecution, led by Los Angeles Deputy District Attorney Pamela Bozanich, wasted no time in presenting a brutal, clear-cut narrative. They contended that the brothers' actions were driven by nothing more than greed. José and Kitty Menendez, wealthy and successful, had amassed a fortune that their sons stood to inherit. According to the prosecution, this wealth was a siren song too alluring for Lyle and Erik to resist. Rather than waiting for their inheritance, the prosecution argued, the brothers chose to expedite their fortune, methodically planning and executing their parents in a cold, calculated bid for freedom and financial independence. They pointed to the brothers' behavior in the aftermath of the murders—the lavish spending spree, the luxury purchases, the parties—as evidence of their lack of remorse, their willingness to celebrate the deaths of the very people who had provided them with the lifestyle they so readily embraced.

The prosecution's approach was meticulous and strategic. They presented evidence of the brothers' expenditures, painting a picture of two young men unburdened by grief, indulging in the spoils of their parents' wealth with an enthusiasm that seemed almost celebratory. Witnesses were called to testify about Lyle and Erik's behavior in the weeks following the murders, each testimony adding to the image of two men whose actions were incongruent with that of grieving sons. Financial records were introduced, showcasing the exorbitant sums the brothers had spent on cars, watches, designer clothing, and luxury vacations. To the prosecution, these purchases were not mere coping mechanisms; they were proof of a premeditated motive, a smoking gun that pointed directly at their guilt.

Bozanich hammered this point home with a relentless focus on motive. She argued that the brothers saw their parents not as family but as obstacles to their freedom. José's strict, overbearing personality, once considered by many as a hallmark of a driven father, was recast by the prosecution as fuel for resentment. Bozanich contended that the brothers' impatience and entitlement had transformed this resentment into murderous intent. With each piece of evidence, each witness, the prosecution sought to cement the narrative of Lyle and Erik as ruthless, selfish individuals who had taken the ultimate step to secure a life unencumbered by parental control.

But the defense, led by the passionate and formidable Leslie Abramson, offered a narrative that was profoundly different—and far more disturbing. Abramson was known for her fierce dedication to her clients and her ability to connect emotionally with juries. She approached the case with a sense of urgency, determined to show the world that the Menendez brothers were not the monsters the prosecution portrayed, but rather victims of horrific abuse who had acted out of fear and psychological torment. Abramson's strategy hinged on exposing the hidden life of the Menendez family, a reality concealed beneath the veneer of wealth and success.

In her opening statements, Abramson laid out a chilling story of abuse, detailing how José Menendez had allegedly subjected his sons to years of physical, emotional, and sexual torment. According to Abramson, the Menendez home was not a sanctuary but a prison, where the brothers lived in constant fear of their father's rage and control. She described José as a tyrant who dominated every aspect of his sons' lives, driving them to the brink of psychological collapse. But the most shocking element of her narrative was the allegation of sexual abuse, a claim that would redefine the way the public saw the Menendez brothers.

The courtroom was gripped as Abramson recounted the harrowing details of the abuse, painting a picture of two boys who had grown up isolated, broken, and desperate. Witnesses were called to corroborate the brothers' stories, including family friends and even a cousin who claimed to have known about the abuse for years. Erik, in particular, became a focal point of the defense's strategy, his emotional fragility used to highlight the extent of his trauma. He took the stand, his voice shaking as he recounted experiences that left the courtroom in stunned silence. Abramson argued that the murders were not driven by greed but by a profound sense of fear—fear that José would continue his abuse, fear that their only way to escape was to take the ultimate, irreversible step.

The defense's narrative cast Kitty Menendez in a different light as well. Far from being an innocent victim, Abramson argued that Kitty had been complicit, or at the very least, indifferent to her husband's abuse. According to the defense, Kitty's struggles with depression and addiction had rendered her incapable of protecting her sons, creating a household where fear and suffering went unchecked. The defense used this portrayal of Kitty to underscore the brothers' sense of entrapment, suggesting that they had nowhere to turn, no safe haven within their own family.

As the trial wore on, the battle between prosecution and defense grew increasingly intense. Bozanich countered Abramson's narrative by questioning the credibility of the abuse allegations, arguing that they were exaggerated, if not fabricated, to excuse a premeditated crime. She scrutinized the brothers' testimony, highlighting inconsistencies in their stories and questioning why they had never reported the abuse to authorities or confided in anyone prior to the murders. To the prosecution, the abuse claims were a last-ditch effort to escape accountability, a story concocted to manipulate the jury's emotions and shift focus away from the brothers' greed.

Abramson, undeterred, doubled down on her portrayal of the Menendez brothers as victims. She argued that trauma could explain the inconsistencies in their stories, that their fear and psychological damage had distorted their memories and actions. She painted Erik as a young man who had been broken beyond repair, unable to see any escape other than the drastic measures he had taken. Her arguments were emotional, drawing on the empathy of the jury, urging them to look past the wealth and privilege and see two young men whose lives had been shaped by unimaginable pain.

The courtroom became a battleground, each side wielding evidence, testimony, and emotion like weapons in a war for the jury's belief. The prosecution's narrative of entitlement and greed clashed with the defense's harrowing story of abuse and desperation, leaving the jury—and the public—torn. Each new piece of evidence, each witness testimony, added layers to the case, painting a picture that was both complex and deeply unsettling. The Menendez trial was no longer a straightforward murder case; it had become a referendum on family dynamics, trauma, and the limits of accountability.

As the trial neared its conclusion, the tension in the courtroom was palpable. The jury was left with two drastically different portrayals of the Menendez brothers. On one hand, they could believe the prosecution's case: that Lyle and Erik were entitled sons who had turned to murder to gain financial independence. On the other, they had the defense's narrative of two broken young men who, after years of abuse, felt trapped with no other way to escape their torment. The case was no longer simply about guilt or innocence; it was about understanding motive, about deciding whether the abuse, if it truly occurred, could excuse or at least explain the unthinkable act the brothers had committed.

In the end, the first trial of Lyle and Erik Menendez left a profound impact on the American public. It raised difficult questions about abuse, privilege, and accountability, questions that would haunt the jury and the viewers who had followed every twist and turn. The courtroom became a stage for a story that was equal parts tragedy and horror, a saga of family secrets, betrayal, and the lengths to which individuals will go to reclaim control over their own lives. The trial had no easy answers, only the raw, haunting truth that sometimes, the line between victim and perpetrator is blurred beyond recognition.

Abuse Allegations in the Courtroom

As the first trial of Lyle and Erik Menendez unfolded, the defense's strategy took a dramatic and deeply unsettling turn. Leslie Abramson, the brothers' passionate and relentless attorney, brought to the forefront an angle that would forever change the perception of the case. The Menendez brothers, Abramson argued, were not simply murderers acting out of greed; they were survivors of years of harrowing abuse, young men driven to a breaking point by a lifetime of trauma inflicted by their father. These allegations, shocking and graphic, reshaped the narrative within the courtroom, turning the trial into a dark exploration of family dysfunction, control, and the unseen horrors that can fester behind closed doors.

Abramson's approach was as bold as it was controversial. She asserted that José Menendez, far from being a respected family patriarch, was a tyrant who wielded power over his sons with a terrifying ruthlessness. In opening statements, Abramson painted a picture of a man whose ambition and desire for control knew no limits.

José's success in the business world, she argued, had been mirrored by his dominance within the family, where he demanded absolute obedience from his sons and enforced his will through methods both cruel and devastating. But what truly captured the attention of the jury and the public were the allegations of sexual abuse—a claim so severe and horrifying that it cast the entire case in a new light. According to the defense, José had sexually abused both Lyle and Erik from a young age, using his power to create an environment of fear and submission. Lyle was the first to allegedly endure this abuse, which, according to Abramson, began when he was just a boy. Years later, José turned his attention to Erik, subjecting him to the same horrors that Lyle had silently endured. Abramson argued that this abuse was not a one-time occurrence but an ongoing, systematic exploitation that left deep psychological scars on both brothers. The allegations painted José as a monstrous figure within his own home, a man who hid his cruelty behind a facade of success and respectability.

To support these claims, the defense called numerous witnesses to the stand, including family friends, distant relatives, and even a cousin who claimed to have known about the abuse. The witnesses described behaviors and interactions that, in retrospect, seemed to suggest something was amiss within the Menendez household. Some recalled moments of tension between José and his sons, subtle indicators that hinted at a darker dynamic. Though much of this testimony was circumstantial, it helped to construct a portrait of a household fraught with unspoken suffering and fear.

The defense's most powerful witness, however, was Erik Menendez himself. When he took the stand, the courtroom fell into a tense silence, each person bracing for the details he was about to share. Erik's testimony was raw and emotional, filled with trembling pauses and moments where he seemed to struggle to find words to describe the abuse he claimed to have endured. He recounted, often in graphic and painful detail, the acts that José allegedly forced upon him, moments that left the courtroom in shock. Erik spoke not just of the physical violation, but of the psychological torment that accompanied it—the sense of powerlessness, the feeling that he had no escape, and the fear that his father's influence would control him for the rest of his life.

Erik's vulnerability on the stand added weight to the defense's narrative. Here was a young man, visibly haunted by his past, openly sharing memories that were as humiliating as they were heartbreaking. Abramson used his testimony to argue that Erik's trauma had reached a breaking point, that the accumulated years of abuse and control had finally driven him to a state where he could see no way out other than to end his father's life. The implication was clear: the murders were not a premeditated act of greed, but a desperate response to years of torment. Lyle, too, was painted as a protector, someone who had endured his own abuse in silence and finally took action to protect his younger brother from further harm.

But Abramson's strategy was not without its risks. The allegations of abuse were shocking, but they were also difficult to prove. There were no records, no reports, no witnesses to the alleged acts themselves—only the words of the brothers, words that were now being used to explain a murder that had, by all outward appearances, been motivated by financial gain. The prosecution, led by Pamela Bozanich, seized upon this lack of concrete evidence, arguing that the abuse allegations were a fabrication, a convenient excuse devised to justify the brothers' actions. Bozanich questioned the timing of the allegations, noting that the brothers had never reported the abuse to authorities, friends, or teachers, and that they had only disclosed these claims after they were facing the possibility of a life sentence.

Throughout cross-examinations, Bozanich drilled into the inconsistencies in Erik and Lyle's accounts, highlighting moments where their stories seemed to diverge or where details shifted under scrutiny. She cast doubt on the plausibility of such severe abuse going unnoticed by everyone around them, especially given the brothers' privileged, high-profile upbringing. The prosecution's argument was straightforward: if the abuse had truly been as severe as the brothers claimed, there would be some evidence, some mark left behind other than their words. Bozanich suggested that the defense's narrative was a calculated ploy to manipulate the emotions of the jury, to create sympathy where none was deserved.

The psychological toll on Erik and Lyle was evident. Under the pressure of cross-examination, Erik's emotional state wavered, his composure cracking as he attempted to reconcile his trauma with the narrative presented by the prosecution. Lyle, though more composed, struggled as well, his role as the elder brother, protector, and, allegedly, the first victim weighed heavily on him. Their testimonies, raw and unfiltered, provided the jury with an intimate glimpse into their minds—yet, whether those testimonies were genuine accounts of abuse or performances designed to elicit sympathy became the central question.

Outside the courtroom, the public was equally divided. Media coverage had turned the trial into a national event, with commentators and experts debating the validity of the abuse allegations. For some, the story of a successful, powerful father who secretly abused his children resonated as a plausible, if horrifying, reality. Others saw the allegations as a cynical defense strategy, a means to justify an act of unthinkable betrayal. The trial, once focused on the question of who had committed the murders, had evolved into a referendum on family trauma, privilege, and the psychological scars left by abusive power dynamics.

Ultimately, the abuse allegations became the defining element of the trial, transforming the brothers from privileged heirs to potential survivors of unspeakable horror. Abramson's relentless focus on the psychological damage inflicted by José aimed to create reasonable doubt, to make the jury question whether these young men, after years of torment, could have truly acted with the clear intent the prosecution argued. It was a battle of empathy versus evidence, a struggle between the plausibility of trauma and the hard facts of the crime.

As the trial reached its conclusion, the jury was left with a profoundly difficult decision. They had to weigh the brothers' testimonies, their visible distress, and the claims of abuse against the prosecution's argument of premeditated, cold-blooded murder. The abuse allegations had humanized Lyle and Erik, revealing young men who, if the defense was to be believed, had endured a life no one should have to bear. Yet, the prosecution's counterpoint—that this was merely a manipulation, a bid for leniency—remained potent.

The courtroom had become a theater of the human psyche, a place where deep-seated traumas and raw emotions were laid bare. In this battle of narratives, neither side held all the answers, and the jury was left with only fragments of a horrifying story, trying to piece together the truth in a case that had shown the world how deeply complex, and deeply disturbing, family bonds could be. The Menendez brothers' trial was no longer just about guilt or innocence; it was about the shadows that can hide within families, and the devastating lengths to which people might go when those shadows are brought into the light.

The Power of Media: Court TV and the National Obsession

As the Menendez brothers' trial unfolded, it became one of the first high-profile cases to be broadcast live on Court TV, capturing the attention of millions across the United States and, ultimately, the world. What might have been a standard court case with closed doors and limited access was transformed into a national spectacle, thanks to the around-the-clock media coverage that brought every witness, every cross-examination, and every emotional breakdown into the living rooms of viewers everywhere. This unprecedented access to the judicial process turned the Menendez brothers' trial into a shared obsession, an engrossing blend of true crime, family drama, and psychological thriller that kept people riveted, day after day, as the shocking details of the Menendez family's tragic story were laid bare.

The advent of Court TV marked a pivotal moment in American media. For the first time, the public could watch a murder trial from start to finish, following along with every twist and turn as if it were a serialized television show. This transparency, hailed by some as a step forward in democratic access to the judicial system, had its darker side as well. The Menendez trial was no longer just a legal proceeding; it was entertainment, and the brothers themselves became unwilling characters in a drama that blurred the lines between reality and spectacle. Television cameras captured their expressions, their body language, and their every reaction, transforming them from defendants into public figures whose lives were dissected with an intensity usually reserved for celebrities.

The story of two young, privileged men accused of brutally murdering their parents in cold blood would have drawn interest on its own, but the layered, complex narratives introduced by both the prosecution and defense made the trial uniquely captivating. With allegations of sexual abuse, family dysfunction, and the struggle for control over a fortune, the Menendez case had all the elements of a soap opera, but with real people, real lives, and real consequences. The public was not merely watching a trial; they were becoming emotionally invested in it, developing opinions and forming allegiances as if the participants were characters in a fiction. Court TV's constant coverage provided an intimate view of the courtroom drama, and soon, Lyle and Erik Menendez were no longer seen just as defendants—they were symbols of familial betrayal, entitlement, and, for some, victimization.

For the defense, led by Leslie Abramson, the media coverage presented both an opportunity and a challenge. Abramson recognized that the story she was telling—the narrative of abuse, desperation, and survival—was one that could resonate deeply with viewers. She knew that if she could sway the public, she could indirectly influence the jury, whose members would be aware of the national debate surrounding the case, no matter how insulated they were supposed to be. Abramson used every opportunity to portray her clients as damaged young men who had been broken by their father's cruelty and control. She delivered her arguments with an emotional intensity that resonated with viewers, building empathy for Lyle and Erik even as the prosecution argued they were nothing more than ruthless killers.

But the media's scrutiny was a double-edged sword. Pamela Bozanich, the prosecutor, also recognized the power of Court TV and the reach of the media. She countered Abramson's narrative by emphasizing the brothers' actions after the murders—their shopping sprees, their attempts to buy status and luxury with their parents' money—as evidence of premeditation and greed. To Bozanich, the image of Lyle and Erik as traumatized victims was a carefully crafted façade, one intended to manipulate both the jury and the watching public. She pointed out the inconsistencies in their stories, the suspicious timing of their abuse allegations, and their seeming lack of remorse, using the courtroom cameras as a tool to reinforce her argument that the Menendez brothers were not broken victims, but entitled killers seeking to escape justice.

Public opinion shifted with each day of the trial, with Court TV's unfiltered access giving the audience the ability to scrutinize every statement, every tear, and every moment of silence. Viewers debated among themselves, split between those who saw the brothers as victims of horrific abuse and those who believed they were cold-blooded murderers exploiting public sympathy. The sheer accessibility of the trial fostered a new kind of viewer participation; audiences felt connected to the case, as though they were part of the process, weighing evidence and testimonies alongside the jury. Across the country, people discussed the case in offices, coffee shops, and homes, dissecting the details and forming opinions as if they, too, were sitting in the jury box.

As the trial progressed, the media's portrayal of the Menendez brothers became increasingly polarized. News outlets produced in-depth profiles of José and Kitty, analyzing their lives, ambitions, and parenting styles, while others published psychological analyses of Lyle and Erik, speculating on the effects of alleged trauma and abuse. Experts, psychologists, and criminal analysts were brought onto television shows to provide insight, each adding another layer to the public's understanding—or misunderstanding—of the case. The Menendez brothers became more than defendants; they were case studies, subjects of fascination and revulsion, and symbols of the complicated dynamics that can exist within families.

Beyond the case itself, the trial's coverage fueled a broader national discussion about family dysfunction, wealth, privilege, and the complex interplay between power and abuse. The Menendez trial forced Americans to confront uncomfortable questions about the pressures of familial expectations, the hidden traumas that can exist even within the most outwardly perfect families, and the lengths people might go to escape unbearable pain. In some ways, the trial acted as a mirror for viewers, reflecting their own anxieties and unresolved tensions about family, control, and loyalty. For some, it became a way to explore societal issues surrounding mental health, trauma, and the impact of power dynamics in relationships. For others, it was simply sensational entertainment, a shocking story that blurred the lines between crime and drama.

Court TV's coverage extended beyond the courtroom, capturing the reactions of the public, legal analysts, and even celebrities who commented on the case. The Menendez brothers' trial was not just on television; it was on talk shows, in newspapers, and on the radio. It was impossible to ignore, and its ubiquity gave it a cultural weight that elevated it beyond a typical criminal case. It became an era-defining moment in media, setting the stage for future cases to receive the same kind of intense, round-the-clock coverage. The O.J. Simpson trial, which followed just a few years later, would benefit from the template established by the Menendez case, proving that Americans had developed an appetite for real-life courtroom drama.

The trial's end left the public divided and exhausted, as people processed the emotional toll of having watched such a brutal, tragic story unfold in real-time. Some felt justice had been served; others believed the brothers' abuse claims, arguing that they had been victims as much as perpetrators. The media's role in shaping public opinion on the Menendez case became a point of reflection, as critics questioned whether the presence of cameras had contributed to a fair trial or turned it into a performance where the stakes were more than just legal.

Ultimately, the Menendez brothers' trial became a case study in the power of media to shape and influence public perception. It was a testament to how easily narratives can be constructed, reframed, and consumed by a public eager for insight into the hidden lives of the rich and powerful. The trial laid bare not only the details of a horrific crime but also the voyeuristic tendencies of a society increasingly accustomed to watching private struggles play out in public. The impact of Court TV's coverage reverberated long after the verdict, as it set a precedent for media in the courtroom and changed the way Americans viewed justice, trauma, and family in the most intimate, unfiltered way possible.

Mistrial and Hung Juries: Public Opinion Shifts

The first trial of Lyle and Erik Menendez, though filled with compelling testimonies, emotional breakdowns, and an unending stream of evidence, ended in a way that left the nation stunned: a mistrial. After months of grueling testimony and intense public scrutiny, the jury was unable to reach a unanimous decision, resulting in a hung jury. This unexpected outcome only deepened the fascination with the case, casting doubt on both the prosecution's certainty and the defense's pleas for sympathy. The mistrial symbolized the profound divide not only within the jury room but also among the American public, who had watched, judged, and debated every detail of the case. Inside the jury deliberations, the division was clear. The defense's allegations of abuse, presented with searing detail and backed by emotionally charged testimonies from Lyle and Erik, had resonated with some jurors. These jurors saw the brothers as victims who had been pushed to a breaking point by years of unimaginable suffering and psychological manipulation. They believed that the abuse, if real, had left the brothers feeling trapped, with no way out except through a tragic act of violence. For these jurors, the murders were less an act of calculated greed and more a desperate attempt to escape the clutches of a tyrannical father.

But other jurors, firmly in the prosecution's camp, saw the brothers as ruthless and calculating. They were not swayed by the claims of abuse, seeing them instead as a last-ditch effort to manipulate the jury's emotions. To them, the brothers' post-murder spending spree and their cold demeanor spoke volumes about their true motivations. The luxury cars, Rolex watches, and other extravagant purchases immediately after their parents' deaths were signs, in their view, not of trauma but of triumph—two young men seizing their inheritance with an eagerness that betrayed any notion of genuine remorse. This jury split made it impossible to reach a verdict, and Judge Stanley Weisberg had no choice but to declare a mistrial.

The public reaction to the hung jury was immediate and intense. People across the country had been captivated by the trial, following every twist and turn with fervent interest. But the mistrial introduced a new wave of opinions, speculation, and debate. Those who sympathized with the Menendez brothers saw the hung jury as validation, proof that the abuse they claimed to have suffered was real and that the legal system was beginning to understand the complexity of their motives. For these supporters, the mistrial represented a step toward recognizing the devastating impact of family abuse, even if it led to extreme actions.

For others, however, the mistrial was an injustice, a failure of the legal system to hold two privileged young men accountable for their crimes. Many were outraged, feeling that the brothers had successfully manipulated the jury through theatrics and fabrications. These critics argued that the abuse allegations were merely a smokescreen, a cleverly crafted story designed to excuse what was, in their eyes, a premeditated and cold-blooded murder. The mistrial left them feeling that justice had been delayed and that the Menendez brothers had escaped a punishment they rightfully deserved.

The split in public opinion reflected broader societal questions about abuse, privilege, and accountability. Some commentators and psychologists appeared on talk shows and news segments to discuss the broader implications of the case. They examined the complexities of abusive family dynamics and the ways in which trauma could distort perceptions, drive behavior, and complicate moral accountability. Others, however, viewed these discussions as a slippery slope, concerned that it might set a dangerous precedent where abuse could be used to justify violent acts. They feared that accepting the brothers' defense would open the door to more cases where defendants might claim abuse as a rationale for criminal behavior, weakening the justice system's ability to impose consequences.

Meanwhile, Court TV continued to fan the flames, replaying key moments from the trial and hosting debates among legal experts, psychologists, and commentators. These televised discussions shaped and reinforced the national debate, as viewers watched clips of Erik's emotional testimony and Lyle's controlled yet impassioned defenses. The discussions revealed just how powerful the court of public opinion had become, as people across the country chose sides based on how they interpreted these televised moments. For many, the Menendez brothers were no longer just defendants—they had become symbols of either familial betrayal or victimhood, each camp projecting its own beliefs and fears onto their story.

As the legal teams prepared for a retrial, public opinion remained as divided as ever. The mistrial had turned the Menendez brothers into household names, figures whose lives and actions were analyzed, dissected, and debated endlessly. People questioned everything—from the truthfulness of their tears to the authenticity of their alleged trauma, and from the motives of their attorneys to the effectiveness of the prosecution's strategy. The case had become a cultural phenomenon, sparking discussions about family, wealth, and the American justice system's ability to discern truth in a world where privilege and pain can so easily intertwine.

For Lyle and Erik, the hung jury was both a relief and a precarious victory. They were aware that the public had taken sides, that their lives were under intense scrutiny, and that the battle was far from over. A retrial loomed, and they knew they would once again have to confront the allegations, the evidence, and the relentless media coverage that had turned their personal tragedy into a national spectacle. With the prospect of a new jury, new testimonies, and possibly even new strategies, the brothers and their legal team braced themselves for another fight, hoping that this time, the verdict might swing in their favor.

For the American public, the mistrial only added to the sense of suspense and drama surrounding the case. They had watched the first trial with fascination, drawn in by the revelations and raw emotions that spilled out in the courtroom. Now, with the promise of a retrial, they knew there would be another chapter, another opportunity to see the Menendez brothers' story play out before their eyes. The Menendez case had become more than just a legal battle; it was a national obsession, a mirror reflecting deep societal anxieties about power, privilege, and the hidden darkness that can lurk within the most outwardly successful families.

As the retrial approached, America remained divided, with each side entrenched in its beliefs about the brothers' innocence or guilt. The case continued to dominate headlines, a media phenomenon that had tapped into the public's appetite for scandal, tragedy, and moral ambiguity. The Menendez brothers, once private individuals, had become public symbols, and the forthcoming retrial promised to reignite the fierce debates that had come to define one of the most sensational criminal cases of the decade. The mistrial was not just a legal outcome; it was a catalyst, ensuring that the story of Lyle and Erik Menendez would linger in the public consciousness for years to come.

Chapter 8: The Second Trial

Restrained Defense: Limited Evidence of Abuse

As the second trial of Lyle and Erik Menendez commenced, the courtroom atmosphere felt noticeably different. The intense, dramatic fervor that had marked the first trial gave way to a somber, almost restrained tone, as if both the legal teams and the public had come to understand the gravity of the case on a deeper level. The brothers, who had once been the center of a media storm and the focal point of a national spectacle, now faced a more controlled and constrained environment. This time, the courtroom was closed off to television cameras, shielding the proceedings from the relentless gaze of the public eye and shifting the focus back to the case itself. For many, this was a relief—a chance for a fairer trial unmarred by the sensationalism of Court TV. For Lyle and Erik, it was a daunting reminder that this time, the spotlight would be focused on the cold facts, and their fate would rest on a jury’s interpretation of evidence presented without the influence of public opinion.

The prosecution, led once again by Deputy District Attorney Pamela Bozanich, came prepared to counter the defense's narrative of abuse that had, in the previous trial, won significant sympathy from certain jurors. But this time, the defense’s strategy would face an uphill battle. Judge Stanley Weisberg, determined to keep the trial more focused and devoid of the emotional manipulation he believed had derailed the first proceedings, imposed severe restrictions on what evidence could be presented regarding the abuse allegations. Unlike the first trial, where the courtroom had been filled with harrowing tales of physical and sexual abuse, the defense would now be limited in the extent to which they could use these claims to explain the brothers' actions.

For Leslie Abramson, Lyle and Erik’s fiercely devoted attorney, the judge’s decision to limit evidence of abuse was a significant setback. The abuse narrative had been her cornerstone argument, a deeply humanizing element that allowed her to present the brothers as victims of unimaginable suffering, driven to violence as a last resort. Without the ability to delve fully into the alleged abuse, Abramson found herself navigating uncharted territory. The defense had to adapt, scaling back its emotionally charged arguments and focusing instead on the psychological impact of the abuse without delving into the explicit details that had captivated the jury during the first trial. The brothers, particularly Erik, would no longer be able to take the stand to tell their stories in vivid, heartbreaking detail—a restriction that fundamentally altered the tone and structure of the defense.

The restrictions placed on the defense meant that Abramson had to take a more clinical approach. She focused on the psychological scars left by years of alleged manipulation, coercion, and control rather than the specific incidents that had marked the brothers' youth. The defense team attempted to build a case around the theory of "battered person syndrome," suggesting that the brothers, after enduring years of mental and emotional degradation, felt that violence was their only means of escape. However, without the deeply personal testimonies and the emotionally charged stories of abuse, this argument lacked the visceral impact it had in the first trial. The brothers' humanity—so carefully constructed through Erik's tearful recounting of his trauma and Lyle's stoic yet anguished presence—was now veiled, muted by the judge's restrictions.

For the jury, this new trial felt more like a detached analysis than an emotionally charged drama. The focus was on timelines, evidence, and psychological theories rather than the personal anguish and heartache that had previously defined the narrative. Witnesses were called, but the testimony was factual, constrained by Judge Weisberg's determination to keep the proceedings focused on the crime itself. The stories that had once painted José Menendez as a tyrannical figure, a father whose control over his sons was absolute, were now presented in fragments, with much of the context removed. Kitty Menendez, who in the first trial had been depicted as a complex figure struggling with her own issues, was now portrayed in simpler terms, as a mother caught in the crossfire of her sons' anger and resentment.

This restrained defense approach affected not only the courtroom dynamics but also the perception of the brothers themselves. Without the lens of abuse coloring every aspect of the trial, Lyle and Erik were once again seen through a more skeptical lens. Gone were the emotional confessions, the tearful admissions of vulnerability; in their place was a more subdued defense that lacked the same emotional resonance. The jury, now shielded from the stories that had evoked empathy in the first trial, was left to evaluate the Menendez brothers on the basis of more objective criteria. This shift forced the defense to rely on psychological experts and clinical testimonies to explain the impact of alleged abuse, transforming the brothers from traumatized young men into subjects of psychological analysis.

The prosecution capitalized on this change in tone, crafting a narrative that stripped away the sympathy evoked by the abuse claims and emphasized the premeditated, calculated nature of the crime. Bozanich argued that the brothers had killed their parents not out of desperation, but out of greed. With the restrictions on abuse testimony, she was able to portray José and Kitty as doting, albeit demanding, parents whose deaths had been orchestrated by sons motivated by financial gain rather than fear. The prosecution's story became simpler, more direct: two young men, accustomed to privilege, had chosen murder as a means to expedite their inheritance. For the jury, this straightforward narrative was compelling and difficult to reconcile with the limited evidence of abuse allowed in the trial.

Outside the courtroom, public interest remained high, even though the media no longer had direct access to the proceedings. The absence of cameras created a sense of mystery around the trial, with the public relying on sketches, written reports, and journalist summaries to glean insight into what was happening behind closed doors. The limitations placed on the defense's abuse narrative also influenced public opinion, which had shifted considerably since the first trial. While some still believed in the brothers' account of a tormented upbringing, others, influenced by the prosecution's simplified portrayal of events, saw them as entitled young men who had resorted to extreme measures for personal gain. The Menendez brothers' supporters, once vocal and visible, became a quieter minority, struggling to maintain their narrative in the face of a more controlled, evidence-based trial.

Throughout the second trial, Lyle and Erik appeared more reserved, their expressions betraying a quiet resignation as they listened to their lives being dissected in clinical terms, devoid of the raw emotion that had once dominated their defense. For them, this new approach was painful; their story, their truth as they saw it, had been diluted, reduced to psychological jargon and theory. They understood that without the full scope of their abuse narrative, the jury might see them in a colder, harsher light—an unbearable thought for two young men who believed they had already lost everything.

The second trial, stripped of its emotional complexity, became an experiment in judicial restraint. By limiting the evidence of abuse, Judge Weisberg had effectively reshaped the entire narrative, pushing both sides to focus on the events of August 20, 1989, as a crime rather than a tragic outcome of family trauma. The jury, guided to examine facts over feelings, was asked to decide if the Menendez brothers were guilty of premeditated murder without the mitigating context that had clouded the first trial. It was a challenge that tested their ability to weigh complex motivations without the benefit of hearing the full, unfiltered story of the Menendez family's dark inner life.

As closing arguments approached, the courtroom was filled with a tense, muted energy. Abramson fought to humanize her clients within the confines of the judge's restrictions, using every tool at her disposal to remind the jury that these were young men shaped by forces beyond their control. But with limited evidence of abuse, her arguments felt less potent, the raw humanity she once so vividly evoked now lost in the sterile language of psychology. For the prosecution, this was a victory—a return to a narrative of accountability, justice, and consequence that they believed the first trial had lacked.

When the jury finally began their deliberations, they were left to sift through two vastly different stories, each obscured by the limitations of the second trial. The narrative of abuse and survival, so central to the defense's case, had been muted, leaving behind a skeletal framework of a story that felt incomplete. The Menendez brothers waited, knowing that this time, the decision would not be influenced by the public or the media, but by a handful of jurors who had witnessed only fragments of their truth.

In the end, the second trial presented the Menendez brothers not as figures of national empathy or horror, but as young men caught in the machinery of justice, their fate determined by what evidence could—and could not—be shown. The final verdict would be a culmination of this stripped-down narrative, a decision made in the stark, restrained silence of a courtroom that had been carefully insulated from the emotional chaos of the first trial. For Lyle and Erik, this verdict would either be their vindication or the end of a long, agonizing journey through the depths of family secrets and public judgment.

Conviction and Sentencing: Life without Parole

As the second trial of Lyle and Erik Menendez drew to a close, the courtroom braced for the final verdict in a case that had transfixed the nation for years. The restrictions imposed on the defense had reshaped the narrative, stripping away much of the emotional resonance that had defined the first trial. Gone were the harrowing testimonies of abuse in vivid detail; instead, the jury was left with a more clinical portrayal of the Menendez family dynamics, guided by timelines, psychological theories, and evidence that was more subdued yet still damning. For Lyle and Erik, this trial was no longer about seeking understanding—it had become a desperate bid to avoid the full weight of the law bearing down on them. But in the end, after days of tense deliberation, the jury reached a conclusion that would seal the brothers' fates.

The courtroom was silent as the jury returned, their faces solemn, each member visibly affected by the burden of deciding the lives of two young men who, at one time, had seemed to have it all. The verdict came swiftly: guilty of first-degree murder for both Lyle and Erik. The jurors had found that the prosecution's portrayal of greed, entitlement, and premeditation outweighed the defense's limited presentation of psychological trauma and abuse. The brothers were convicted on two counts of murder with special circumstances, a verdict that in California meant a mandatory sentence of life in prison without the possibility of parole. It was a decision that resonated with finality, a powerful statement from the justice system that the severity of their crime could not be diminished, regardless of the pain they claimed to have endured.

As the verdict was read, Lyle and Erik sat stoically, their faces betraying little emotion. The quiet resignation they had shown throughout the trial remained, as if they had anticipated this outcome. For months, they had watched as their story was systematically dismantled, as the allegations of abuse that once evoked empathy were subdued into psychological jargon that lacked the visceral impact of their testimonies in the first trial. They knew that this second attempt at justice was proceeding on terms that did not favor them, that the jury had not heard the full extent of the horrors they claimed to have suffered. And now, facing a sentence that would confine them to prison for the rest of their lives, they appeared more resigned than shocked, as though they had already come to terms with the path that lay ahead.

For the defense team, particularly Leslie Abramson, the verdict was a crushing blow. Abramson had fought tirelessly for Lyle and Erik, pushing the boundaries of empathy and law to humanize them as victims. She had believed, wholeheartedly, in the abuse narrative, in the idea that these brothers were damaged souls seeking freedom from a tyrannical father's control. But with Judge Weisberg's restrictions, her arguments had been constrained, her passionate defense muted, leaving her unable to fully convey the depth of suffering she felt justified their actions. In her eyes, justice had not been served; the court had overlooked the trauma that she believed was central to understanding the brothers' motivations. She would go on to appeal the verdict, but the odds were slim, and the finality of the sentence hung heavily in the air.

The sentencing itself was swift and uncompromising: life without the possibility of parole. The judge, in his remarks, emphasized the brutal nature of the crime, highlighting the premeditation and the calculated steps the brothers had taken to ensure their parents' deaths. He spoke of the betrayal, the deliberate planning, and the apparent lack of remorse displayed in the aftermath of the murders. For the court, the narrative of abuse did not mitigate the severity of the crime. Lyle and Erik's actions were viewed not as acts of desperation, but as the ultimate transgression born from entitlement and a desire for freedom, taken at the cost of their parents' lives. Life without parole, he concluded, was the only sentence that could balance the scales of justice in light of the crime's gravity.

Outside the courtroom, the reaction was equally divided. For many who had followed the case closely, the life sentences seemed fitting, a necessary measure of justice for a crime so heinous and cold-blooded. The notion that two sons could murder their own parents, regardless of their upbringing, was unforgivable to these viewers. To them, the brothers had not only taken lives but also violated the most sacred bond—the relationship between parent and child. The life sentences were seen as a relief, a reassurance that the justice system could look beyond the complexities of family trauma and deliver a punishment that fit the crime.

However, others felt a lingering sense of unease, a feeling that the trial had left too many questions unanswered. Advocates for the brothers pointed to the limitations on abuse testimony, arguing that the court had refused to acknowledge the possibility that years of alleged trauma could drive someone to act in ways that defied rational understanding. They believed that the legal restrictions had prevented the jury from truly comprehending the depth of the brothers' suffering, leading to a decision that prioritized punishment over rehabilitation or compassion. For these supporters, the life sentences felt harsh, a denial of the nuanced realities of abuse and psychological damage that might explain—if not justify—their actions.

The Menendez brothers were transported from the courtroom to begin their sentences, each now facing the stark reality of a life spent behind bars. The media continued to follow their story, chronicling their adjustments to prison life, their attempts to find purpose within the confines of their sentences, and their connections to the outside world. Over the years, they would both find companionship, marrying women who believed in their innocence or felt a connection to their story. They pursued education, engaged in prison programs, and worked to carve out lives within the restrictions of their circumstances. But the weight of the life sentence remained, a constant reminder of the brutal decision they had made and the irrevocable consequences it carried.

For the American public, the Menendez case would endure as one of the most notorious family crimes in modern history—a dark cautionary tale about privilege, family dynamics, and the lengths people might go to escape unbearable situations. The life sentences underscored society's need for accountability, a stark message that no amount of familial dysfunction could excuse such violence. Yet, for many, the case also sparked an ongoing dialogue about trauma, abuse, and the complexities of mental health in the criminal justice system. The Menendez brothers' life sentences represented more than just justice served; they reflected the societal struggle to reconcile compassion with accountability, empathy with the rule of law.

Reactions and Reflections: A Nation Divided

The conviction and life sentences of Lyle and Erik Menendez left America both riveted and divided, sparking heated debates that extended well beyond the courtroom walls. The Menendez case had captured the nation's attention from the start, but the finality of the verdict—and the sentence of life without parole—evoked a wide spectrum of emotions. For many, the Menendez brothers' sentencing represented a triumph of justice, an assertion of society's unwavering stance against patricide. For others, however, the outcome was troubling, raising complex moral and ethical questions about the justice system's handling of trauma and abuse. As the dust settled, the nation found itself wrestling with these opposing views, divided by the nuances and contradictions inherent in a case that defied simple explanations.

For those who supported the verdict, the sentences offered closure. In their eyes, Lyle and Erik were not victims but perpetrators of a cold, calculated crime. These Americans viewed the defense's claims of abuse with skepticism, seeing them as a convenient narrative crafted to evade accountability. The brothers' lavish spending spree following the murders, their seemingly emotionless response to their parents' deaths, and the carefully orchestrated lies they had told the police painted a picture of two young men who acted not out of desperation, but out of entitlement. To supporters of the verdict, the Menendez brothers' sentence of life without parole was a necessary outcome, a message that privilege does not exempt one from responsibility. They felt justice had been served, and that the brothers, despite their upbringing, were ultimately responsible for their actions.

This view was shared by much of the mainstream media, which framed the Menendez brothers as the epitome of "affluenza"—privileged young men who, accustomed to getting everything they wanted, resorted to murder to liberate themselves from perceived constraints. Commentators who championed this perspective argued that allowing the abuse claims to excuse or even mitigate the murders would set a dangerous precedent, one that could invite future defendants to exploit trauma narratives to justify heinous acts. For them, the trial was a reaffirmation of the justice system's role in holding individuals accountable, regardless of their personal histories. They saw the life sentences as both a deterrent and a moral stand, an affirmation of society's stance against the severest breaches of familial bonds.

However, a significant portion of the public felt that the justice system had failed to address the complexity of the Menendez brothers' circumstances. For these individuals, the brothers' lives—mired in alleged abuse, manipulation, and control—painted a portrait of trauma that could not simply be ignored. Supporters of the brothers believed that the abuse claims, though restricted in the second trial, were credible and deeply relevant to understanding why Lyle and Erik might have resorted to such extreme measures. To them, the courtroom restrictions that limited the defense's ability to share the full extent of the brothers' suffering created an incomplete picture, one that leaned heavily in favor of the prosecution's narrative of greed and entitlement. This side of the public argued that the trial's outcome reflected a broader societal failure to acknowledge the psychological impacts of trauma, especially within family systems that can remain hidden from public view.

This sentiment was echoed by mental health advocates, psychologists, and activists who saw the Menendez case as emblematic of the justice system's inadequacies in handling cases involving abuse. Many argued that the life sentences ignored the potential for rehabilitation and healing, instead confining two young men to a life of incarceration without any consideration of the circumstances that shaped them. They viewed the brothers' actions as tragic but understandable responses to years of psychological manipulation and control, seeing their fate as a missed opportunity to explore restorative justice. For these advocates, the case highlighted a need for more nuanced approaches within the legal system that could incorporate a deeper understanding of trauma and its long-lasting effects on mental health.

The divided public opinion also extended to family members, former friends, and acquaintances of the

Menendez family. Some who had known the family expressed surprise and dismay at the allegations of abuse, finding it difficult to reconcile the public image of José Menendez as a successful, driven father with the picture painted by the defense. Yet, others close to the family hinted that José's strict and controlling nature was well-known and that the brothers' claims, though shocking, might not have been entirely fabricated. These differing perspectives within the family and social circles mirrored the broader national divide, reflecting the complicated nature of the Menendez family dynamics and the difficulty of fully understanding what transpired behind closed doors.

As the years passed, the Menendez brothers themselves became a source of intrigue, further complicating public opinion. From within their prison walls, both Lyle and Erik showed signs of personal growth. They pursued educational opportunities, took on leadership roles within the prison community, and, remarkably, each found love and married while incarcerated. Their seemingly genuine efforts to build lives of meaning within the confines of their sentences led some to question whether the brothers were truly beyond redemption. To their supporters, these signs of maturity and change reinforced the belief that the Menendez brothers deserved a chance for parole—an opportunity to prove that their actions, while abhorrent, were born from circumstances beyond their control and that they had transformed since that tragic night.

This nuanced view of the Menendez case was amplified in recent years by a resurgence of interest in true crime, with documentaries, articles, and podcasts re-examining the circumstances surrounding the murders. The reanalysis of evidence, testimonies, and the psychological profiles of the brothers offered new generations a chance to engage with the case, often leading to a more sympathetic understanding of Lyle and Erik. Social media platforms became hotbeds for debate, with younger audiences, in particular, questioning the fairness of the trial and the justice system's handling of abuse claims. In a cultural climate more attuned to mental health and trauma, these newer voices often leaned toward seeing the Menendez brothers as victims of their environment, trapped in a cycle of familial control and psychological abuse.

Ultimately, the Menendez case became more than just a high-profile murder trial; it became a mirror reflecting America's ongoing struggle to reconcile justice with compassion. The case forced the nation to confront difficult questions: Can trauma ever justify violence? Should the legal system incorporate psychological and social factors into sentencing for severe crimes? Is there a path to redemption for those who have committed the most unforgivable acts? These questions lingered long after the verdict, fueling debates that would continue for decades and inspiring legal discussions about how to handle cases involving abuse, privilege, and accountability.

In the end, the life sentences without the possibility of parole stood as the final word in the Menendez brothers' legal saga. But the court's decision did little to silence the public discourse or resolve the complexities of their story. For some, Lyle and Erik remain privileged young men who acted out of greed, their punishment a fitting conclusion to a crime that shocked the conscience of the nation. For others, they are tragic figures, haunted by a lifetime of trauma, whose actions, while unforgivable, merited a more compassionate approach.

Today, the Menendez case endures as a stark reminder of the limits of the justice system, the impact of media sensationalism, and the complex, often painful nature of family bonds. The nation remains divided, each side holding fast to its interpretation of who Lyle and Erik Menendez truly are—monsters born of privilege or victims of a father's tyranny—and whether the sentences they received were justice served or justice denied.

Part V:

Life in Prison

Chapter 9: Surviving Prison

The Brothers' Early Experiences Behind Bars

When Lyle and Erik Menendez entered the prison system to begin their life sentences without the possibility of parole, the enormity of their situation settled in with a chilling finality. No amount of preparation could fully brace them for the abrupt transition from life as sons of privilege in Beverly Hills to the harsh, unyielding reality of a high-security prison. The gates clanged shut behind them, marking not only the end of a sensational trial but also the beginning of a life where every hour, every movement, would be dictated by the rhythms and rules of incarceration. For the Menendez brothers, this was the first step in a journey of survival—a journey that would force them to adapt, transform, and find a sense of purpose within the confines of their new world.

The initial months behind bars were brutal for both brothers, physically and psychologically. Lyle and Erik, who had lived in comfort, now faced the harsh, unfiltered atmosphere of prison life. They were no longer insulated by wealth or status; their identities, once shaped by privilege, had been stripped down to the barest essentials. Inmates viewed them with a mix of suspicion, curiosity, and hostility. The notorious nature of their case preceded them, and the details of their crime—a patricide rooted in wealth, power, and alleged abuse—fueled a potent blend of fascination and disdain among fellow prisoners. In this unfamiliar environment, they quickly understood that their past lives held no currency; instead, they would need to prove their resilience, their adaptability, and, above all, their ability to endure.

Separated in different facilities, Lyle and Erik experienced isolation in profound ways. Each brother faced the challenge of prison life without the support of the other—a cruel irony given the dependence and bond that had shaped their actions, their trial, and their entire lives. They were forced to navigate the intricacies of prison society alone, each facing the daily trials of survival as individuals rather than as the united front they had once presented to the world. Erik, who had always been more emotionally vulnerable, struggled deeply with the loss of connection. He found himself battling waves of depression and despair, haunted by guilt and the overwhelming loneliness that prison fostered. Lyle, though outwardly more stoic, felt the weight of isolation as well, his mind relentlessly replaying the choices and actions that had led them to this fate.

Prison life brought challenges that neither of them could have anticipated. Lyle and Erik were accustomed to a world of comfort and ease; prison, by contrast, was an environment where survival depended on strength, adaptability, and the ability to navigate complex social hierarchies. In the early months, they faced intimidation, altercations, and the perpetual undercurrent of threat that permeated life behind bars. The prison environment was one of rigid codes, unwritten rules, and shifting allegiances—a reality where respect was hard-won and easily lost, and where vulnerability could quickly make one a target. For Lyle and Erik, survival required a recalibration of everything they had once known about human interaction. They were no longer the sons of a powerful executive; here, they were just two more inmates, each struggling to find their place within the system.

As they began to adapt, Lyle and Erik sought ways to make sense of their new existence. Each found different ways to cope, gradually forging paths that would allow them to endure the psychological toll of a life sentence. Lyle turned his attention toward structure and discipline, seeking roles within the prison that would give him a sense of purpose. He became involved in prison jobs, volunteered for various responsibilities, and attempted to establish a semblance of order in his life. These roles offered him a way to focus his energy, providing a distraction from the overwhelming reality of his situation. By throwing himself into these duties, Lyle began to carve out a small niche for himself, one that granted him a modicum of respect among fellow inmates and allowed him to regain some control over his daily life.

Erik, on the other hand, leaned into introspection and personal growth. He sought solace in education, enrolling in classes and dedicating himself to learning. Education became both an escape and a lifeline, giving him something to hold onto as he grappled with the trauma and guilt that lingered from his past. The pursuit of knowledge, along with occasional involvement in religious and therapeutic programs, gave Erik a sense of direction that helped him navigate the darkest moments of his incarceration. In time, he became involved in support groups, particularly those focused on coping with trauma, seeking to address the psychological wounds that had festered long before the crime that had come to define him. Erik's journey was one of healing as much as it was survival, an attempt to come to terms with his past while building a future within the narrow parameters allowed by his sentence.

For both brothers, the challenge was not only to survive but to find meaning within an existence that seemed devoid of it. Their identities had been irrevocably changed, reshaped by the confines of prison life and the notoriety of their crime. They understood that redemption, in the eyes of the world, might forever elude them. Yet, within the walls of their respective prisons, they each sought a sense of personal redemption—a way to rebuild fragments of their humanity amidst the endless monotony and underlying violence of prison life. Their survival became an act of quiet resilience, an acceptance of their fate paired with a commitment to reclaim whatever pieces of themselves they could salvage.

As the years passed, the Menendez brothers continued to adapt, each building a life that, while limited, held elements of stability and routine. The early challenges of intimidation and isolation were replaced by the rhythms of prison life, a world where days blurred into years and survival transformed into acceptance. Though they remained separated by the prison system, they found ways to stay connected through letters, each one a reminder of the bond that had survived even their darkest decisions. In the limited ways available to them, Lyle and Erik managed to build lives within the prison walls, establishing a fragile peace amidst the unyielding reality of their sentences.

Adaptation and Rehabilitation Efforts

As the years in prison wore on, Lyle and Erik Menendez began to reshape their lives within the confines of the system, transitioning from mere survival to adaptation and a pursuit of personal growth. Confronted daily by the harsh reality of their sentences—life without the possibility of parole—they each sought ways to reclaim a sense of purpose, piecing together new identities in a world defined by bars, schedules, and restrictions. Over time, the brothers embarked on a journey of adaptation and rehabilitation, not in a bid for freedom, but as a means of finding peace within the permanent bounds of their confinement.

Lyle, ever the pragmatist, approached rehabilitation through structure, discipline, and leadership. He found his footing in the prison's various job programs, taking on roles that granted him responsibilities and, in turn, respect from both inmates and staff. Working in the prison's administrative functions, he utilized organizational skills that echoed the ambition and drive he had inherited from his father. These positions gave Lyle a sense of agency that had been stripped away upon his incarceration, allowing him to exert control over his immediate environment. Through these roles, he gained a degree of trust and authority, positioning himself as a dependable figure among his peers.

In addition to his work, Lyle became involved in the inmate government at Mule Creek State Prison, where he spent much of his sentence before being transferred to join Erik at the Richard J. Donovan Correctional Facility. His leadership role allowed him to advocate for changes that could improve the quality of life for those around him, from petitioning for better recreational equipment to helping organize educational and vocational programs. This involvement wasn't just an effort to fill his time; it was a way to serve a purpose larger than himself, to make meaningful contributions within the limited scope of prison life. For Lyle, this leadership became a lifeline, a way to channel his energy productively and to engage in a form of community service within the prison walls.

Erik, on the other hand, approached rehabilitation from a more introspective angle. His initial years in prison were marked by bouts of depression and self-reflection, haunted by guilt and the psychological scars he had carried since childhood. But over time, he found solace in education and therapy, using these resources as tools to better understand himself and come to terms with the trauma that had, in his mind, shaped his life and actions. Erik enrolled in various educational courses, earning certificates and expanding his knowledge in subjects ranging from psychology to religious studies. Education became a form of mental and emotional escape, a pathway to growth that allowed him to transcend, in some small way, the boundaries of his cell. Therapy and group counseling sessions also played a significant role in Erik's rehabilitation efforts. He became involved in groups aimed at helping inmates process their trauma and build emotional resilience, a stark contrast to the combative, hostile environment that characterized much of prison life. Erik's participation in these groups evolved over time, from a recipient of counseling to a facilitator who helped others manage their own struggles with mental health. His involvement in these programs was not merely therapeutic but also transformative, marking a shift from self-centered introspection to empathy and support for those around him. In his sessions, Erik shared openly about his own experiences, using his story to create a space of mutual understanding and healing for others.

In time, both Lyle and Erik grew committed to promoting rehabilitation efforts within their respective facilities. The brothers took on mentoring roles, guiding younger inmates who entered the system, many of whom had backgrounds marked by abuse, poverty, and violence. Lyle, with his leadership experience, became a steadying presence for those who struggled to adapt to the strict and often volatile world of prison. He offered advice, encouragement, and a listening ear, creating a sense of camaraderie and solidarity among inmates who viewed him as someone who understood the challenges of confinement. Through mentorship, Lyle not only served others but also solidified his own sense of purpose, channeling his energy into the well-being of those around him.

Erik's Work with Terminally Ill Inmates and Religious Studies

Erik, too, found a form of redemption in mentoring, particularly with inmates facing end-of-life care. At one point, he worked alongside terminally ill inmates, providing companionship and comfort to those who had no family or friends to support them. The role forced Erik to confront mortality in a way that was both humbling and enlightening, a chance to contribute positively within the constraints of prison. He found a kind of peace in offering comfort to others, recognizing that even in the darkest moments, there was an opportunity to connect and to show compassion. This work, along with his involvement in religious and spiritual studies, marked Erik's ongoing journey toward self-acceptance and healing—a path that allowed him to make amends within the confines of his reality.

The transfer of Lyle to Richard J. Donovan Correctional Facility in 2018 brought the brothers together for the first time in over two decades, marking a pivotal moment in their rehabilitation journeys. Once housed in separate facilities, their reunion provided a rare opportunity to reconnect, offering mutual support that added strength to each of their efforts. In many ways, the reunion revitalized their commitment to their individual and shared paths of self-improvement. Together, they collaborated on projects aimed at enhancing the prison community, such as painting a mural on the walls of their shared recreational yard. The mural became a symbol of their resilience, a creative outlet that allowed them to contribute something positive and lasting to the lives of those around them.

The brothers' adaptation to prison life and their commitment to rehabilitation did not erase their past, nor did it garner universal forgiveness. Their crimes, seared into the collective memory of the public, were not easily forgotten. But within the prison system, their efforts to reform and contribute had earned them a degree of respect and acceptance. Lyle and Erik's transition from notorious inmates to mentors and advocates was a testament to the power of rehabilitation, a quiet assertion that growth is possible even within the confines of life without parole.

Their transformation underscored the potential for resilience and change in even the most confined and restricted environments.

In the eyes of their fellow inmates, Lyle and Erik were no longer just the infamous Menendez brothers; they had become part of the prison community, figures who had found ways to navigate their reality with dignity, purpose, and compassion. Though society at large may never forgive or forget their actions, within the walls of their correctional facility, they were seen as individuals who had faced their past, taken responsibility, and dedicated themselves to lives of constructive contribution. In an existence that offered few choices, they had chosen growth over despair, and adaptation over resignation, using their rehabilitation efforts to redefine themselves as more than the sum of their darkest deeds.

For Lyle and Erik, the journey of rehabilitation was ongoing—a daily commitment to finding meaning within the stark limits of prison life, a pursuit of personal redemption in a world that, outside of those walls, might never see them as anything more than the brothers who killed their parents. Yet within that narrow world, they had become men with purpose, dedicated to fostering a community where others, too, might find ways to heal, adapt, and endure. Their transformation served as a reminder that even in the bleakest circumstances, humanity can persist, and the potential for change remains a quiet, resilient force.

As Erik Menendez settled into life behind bars, he began to seek not only a path of personal growth but also a way to give back, to find meaning within the stark limits of his sentence. It was through work with terminally ill inmates and a deepening involvement in religious studies that Erik found a sense of purpose that extended beyond himself. The work was both emotionally challenging and profoundly transformative, pushing Erik to confront issues of mortality, compassion, and forgiveness in a way that allowed him to reconcile parts of his own troubled past. In many ways, these acts of service and his spiritual journey became an avenue for Erik to make peace with the life he would lead behind prison walls—a life marked by irrevocable loss, but one where he could still offer comfort and guidance to those around him.

When Erik first began working with terminally ill inmates, he was faced with the brutal realities of life and death within the prison system. Many of these men had no family to visit them, no friends to hold their hands or offer solace in their final days. Their deaths were often quiet, unremarked upon by the outside world, their suffering largely unseen. Erik stepped into this role with a solemn commitment, seeing in it a chance to bring humanity to a place that so often felt devoid of it. He sat with these men, listened to their stories, and offered companionship in their final moments—a simple act of presence that, for many, provided a small but significant sense of peace.

Through this work, Erik experienced a humbling empathy that he had seldom felt before. He listened to the regrets, hopes, and fears of men who, like him, were trapped by their choices and circumstances. Some of these inmates had also committed serious crimes, and their confessions to Erik, spoken in quiet, reflective tones, created an unspoken bond between them. They were men defined by their pasts but facing the ultimate end with a vulnerability that cut through the walls they had each built around their lives. For Erik, these moments illuminated the fragility of the human spirit, the importance of compassion, and the realization that redemption, while elusive, could be found in small acts of kindness and humility.

Erik's work with terminally ill inmates was not just a service to others but a journey of self-discovery and healing for himself. Being present with others as they faced death made him confront his own life, his own choices, and the weight of the actions that had brought him to this point. Witnessing the end of life so closely allowed Erik to examine what it truly meant to live with intention, even within the restrictions of prison. He found that by giving to others, he was also healing parts of himself, addressing the guilt and remorse that had haunted him since the murder of his parents. This role gave him purpose, a reason to get up each day with the knowledge that he could make a difference, even in the smallest ways. It was a quiet, steadying influence that helped him find peace amid the turbulence of incarceration.

Parallel to his work with terminally ill inmates, Erik immersed himself in religious studies, seeking solace and understanding through spirituality. Initially, his engagement with religion was tentative, an exploration driven by a desire for comfort and answers. But as he delved deeper, Erik found himself drawn into the teachings and the sense of community that religious study provided. He participated in Bible studies, attended prayer groups, and spent hours reading scripture, searching for guidance and a framework within which he could understand his actions, his past, and his future. Religious studies became more than just a ritual for Erik; it was a lifeline, a means of finding forgiveness for himself and understanding his purpose in life, even as that life would be lived out behind prison walls.

Through his studies, Erik began to reflect on the concepts of forgiveness, redemption, and accountability. He struggled with the weight of his actions, grappling with how he could ask for forgiveness from a world he had so deeply hurt. Religious teachings offered him a pathway—not to absolution in the eyes of society, but to an inner peace that allowed him to accept his humanity, flaws and all. He found solace in the idea of grace, the belief that one could be forgiven even when redemption seemed impossible. This belief did not erase his guilt but transformed it into a source of motivation, encouraging him to live each day in a way that honored the value of compassion, humility, and service to others.

Over time, Erik became more active in sharing his faith with other inmates, leading small study groups and discussions on spirituality and personal growth. He wasn't preaching or attempting to convert others but rather opening a space for dialogue, a place where inmates could explore their own beliefs and struggles. Erik shared his journey openly, speaking about the challenges of self-forgiveness and the difficult path toward acceptance. His vulnerability and willingness to engage in these discussions garnered him respect within the prison community, as other inmates began to view him not just as the "Menendez brother" but as someone who understood suffering and the search for redemption on a personal level.

In these roles—counselor to the dying and spiritual guide to the lost—Erik found a kind of rebirth. He had been stripped of his former identity, his life as the privileged son of José and Kitty Menendez, and left to confront the person he had become. Prison forced him to examine his choices with brutal honesty, to face the consequences of his actions, and to rebuild his life from a place of deep humility. Through his work with terminally ill inmates and his religious studies, Erik began to forge a new identity rooted in empathy, compassion, and faith. This journey didn't absolve him of his past, nor did it lessen the weight of the crime he had committed. But it allowed him to find meaning in a life where meaning seemed impossible, offering him a path forward within the restrictive boundaries of his sentence.

For Erik, this spiritual journey and his work with those at the end of their lives became a testament to his transformation. The man who entered prison was lost, consumed by guilt, shame, and confusion. But through years of reflection, service, and study, he found a way to navigate the darkness of his existence with a sense of purpose. While he would never be free in the physical sense, Erik had, in his own way, found a form of inner liberation—a peace that came from knowing he was using his time to bring comfort to others and to pursue a path of faith and humility.

The work Erik did with terminally ill inmates and his engagement in religious studies redefined his life behind bars. It reshaped his purpose, grounded him in compassion, and offered a vision of redemption that, while not public, was deeply personal. For Erik Menendez, these efforts symbolized a commitment to living meaningfully, even within the confines of his punishment—a commitment to finding light in the darkness, one small act of kindness at a time.

Lyle's Leadership in Prison Reform and Inmate Government

While Erik found solace and purpose in spiritual pursuits and working with terminally ill inmates, Lyle Menendez channeled his energy into tangible, systemic change within the prison environment. Known for his organizational skills and pragmatic approach, Lyle carved out a role in the inmate government, where he quickly rose as a respected leader and advocate for reform. His work wasn't just about survival; it was about creating a more humane and constructive prison environment for everyone around him. Over time, he became a driving force in the prison community, using his position and influence to initiate reforms, advocate for inmates' rights, and foster a sense of order and purpose in a setting that was often chaotic and harsh.

Lyle's involvement in inmate government began humbly, with minor roles that offered him an opportunity to engage in the daily operations of prison life. He was first assigned responsibilities within the inmate council, a body that acted as a liaison between inmates and prison administration. Here, Lyle learned the intricacies of prison policies and the often-overlooked issues that affected the daily lives of incarcerated men. Over time, his natural leadership qualities emerged, and he gained the respect of both fellow inmates and staff. Through his work, Lyle developed a nuanced understanding of the challenges within the prison system, from overcrowding to limited access to educational and recreational programs, which inspired him to take a proactive role in pushing for improvements.

As his reputation grew, Lyle was elected to represent his housing unit in inmate government, giving him a larger platform to voice concerns and propose changes. Recognizing that prison life was rife with tension, violence, and a lack of productive engagement, Lyle focused his efforts on initiatives that promoted rehabilitation and community-building. He pushed for increased access to educational programs, arguing that providing inmates with learning opportunities could reduce recidivism and improve overall morale. His advocacy for vocational training and academic courses aimed to give inmates skills they could use to rebuild their lives if they ever re-entered society. Even for those serving life sentences, Lyle believed that education was a form of empowerment, a way to instill purpose and self-worth within the confines of prison walls.

One of Lyle's notable achievements in the realm of prison reform was his advocacy for mental health resources. Through his own experiences and those of the men around him, he saw firsthand the mental toll that incarceration took on individuals. Depression, anxiety, and unresolved trauma were rampant, yet resources for mental health care were often scarce. Lyle used his position to negotiate for improved mental health services, requesting additional counselors and therapy options for inmates struggling with their psychological well-being. Although change was slow and resources limited, his persistence led to small yet meaningful improvements, making it easier for inmates to access counseling and peer support groups.

In addition to promoting education and mental health initiatives, Lyle also worked to reduce violence within the prison. Understanding that much of the aggression stemmed from underlying frustrations and a lack of structure, he advocated for increased recreational activities and job programs that would allow inmates to channel their energy constructively. His efforts helped establish more regular access to the prison gym, recreational fields, and art classes, providing a creative outlet for those who might otherwise turn to violence out of boredom or despair. The presence of these programs created a noticeable shift in the atmosphere, fostering a sense of community and cooperation that helped mitigate conflicts. For Lyle, these initiatives weren't just about improving day-to-day life; they were a means of creating a safer, more supportive environment where inmates could find purpose and stability.

Lyle's leadership also extended to working closely with prison administrators to advocate for fair treatment of inmates. He took on the role of mediator during disputes between inmates and staff, using his position to address grievances and find solutions that respected the rights of both parties. His diplomatic approach and dedication to building trust with prison officials led to open lines of communication that facilitated a more collaborative relationship between the inmate council and the administration. By fostering mutual respect, Lyle helped to create a climate where grievances could be aired and addressed without escalating into hostility or punitive measures. His work in this area established him as a bridge between two often-opposing worlds—the inmates and the institution—allowing him to advocate for fair policies and a more humane approach to prison management.

In time, Lyle's advocacy for reform extended beyond the immediate needs of his fellow inmates. He became involved in larger discussions about prison reform, seeking ways to bring the issue of humane incarceration practices into the public conversation. He wrote letters to organizations focused on prison reform and occasionally worked with advocacy groups that supported educational and rehabilitative initiatives within the prison system. Though his influence was limited by his life sentence, Lyle's insights and experiences as an inmate leader contributed to a broader understanding of the importance of reform, especially in an era where criminal justice was beginning to face closer scrutiny from policymakers and the public.

Perhaps one of Lyle's most enduring contributions was his mentorship of younger inmates. Having seen the consequences of poor choices and a lack of direction, Lyle dedicated himself to guiding others who entered the prison system without a sense of purpose. He counseled young men who were struggling to adjust, offering them advice on how to survive and make the most of their time in prison. Many of these younger inmates viewed Lyle as a father figure or a mentor, someone who had found stability and dignity within the harsh environment of incarceration. Through these relationships, Lyle built a legacy of support and resilience, helping others to navigate their own struggles and avoid the pitfalls that often led to violence and despair.

For Lyle Menendez, his role in inmate government and prison reform became a source of identity that transcended his infamous past. In a setting where hope was scarce and life was defined by confinement, his efforts to promote education, reduce violence, and improve mental health resources offered him a path to redemption. While he knew that society might never forgive him, he found a way to forgive himself by dedicating his life to helping others. His contributions were a testament to the possibility of transformation, even in the most restrictive environments—a reminder that personal growth and positive change could arise from the darkest of circumstances.

In his own quiet way, Lyle Menendez became a beacon of resilience and reform within the prison system. His leadership, though constrained by the physical confines of his sentence, reached far beyond the walls of his cell. Through his work, he demonstrated that individuals, regardless of their past, could contribute meaningfully to their communities, even under the most challenging conditions. His commitment to making prison life more humane, purposeful, and constructive left an indelible mark on those around him and offered a glimpse of what prison reform could look like if approached with empathy, dignity, and a focus on rehabilitation over punishment.

Years Apart: Attempts to Reunite

For years after their sentencing, Lyle and Erik Menendez lived their prison lives separated by hundreds of miles, each confined to a different correctional facility within California's sprawling prison system. This physical distance compounded the emotional isolation they already felt, and despite their deep bond, the brothers' communication was reduced to letters and, occasionally, brief phone calls. Having shared not only their childhood and upbringing but also the trauma of their parents' murder, the trial, and the public scrutiny that followed, the separation was a cruel reminder of their new reality. Both brothers longed for a reunion, to have the solace of family—even in the limited, regimented way that prison could allow—but achieving this goal proved a long, arduous process.

Lyle and Erik's attempts to reunite began almost immediately after their incarceration. They appealed to prison officials, requesting transfer to the same facility. Yet, their high-profile status and the nature of their crime presented unique challenges. Prison authorities were hesitant to house them together due to concerns over security and the potential for the brothers to collaborate in any escape attempts. This separation was also part of a longstanding policy within the California Department of Corrections and Rehabilitation (CDCR), which often kept co-defendants and family members separated to avoid any complications that could arise from their close association. For years, Lyle and Erik persisted, submitting formal requests, writing letters, and even appealing to external organizations that advocated for inmate rights. Their requests were denied time and again, and the prospect of reuniting seemed to grow dimmer as the years wore on. Each denial was a blow to their morale, underscoring the severity of their punishment—not only were they confined for life, but they were also deprived of the one person who might bring a semblance of familial support and comfort to their lives behind bars. Despite these setbacks, both brothers remained hopeful and continued to press for their transfer, convinced that if they could simply be in the same facility, they could face their reality with greater strength.

In 2013, there was a glimmer of hope when Erik was transferred to Richard J. Donovan Correctional Facility, a medium-security prison located in San Diego. This was closer to Lyle than before, but he remained incarcerated at Mule Creek State Prison in northern California, meaning they were still hundreds of miles apart. The change in Erik's location reinvigorated their attempts to reunite. Lyle, in particular, wrote to prison officials and advocates, appealing for a transfer to Donovan. He argued that their separation served no rehabilitative purpose and that their reunion could provide mutual emotional support, a small mercy within the otherwise grueling conditions of life imprisonment.

Then, in February 2018, after more than two decades of separation, Lyle's transfer request was finally granted. He was moved to the same facility as Erik, arriving at Richard J. Donovan Correctional Facility, where the two brothers now shared not only a prison yard but, for the first time in over 20 years, the opportunity for face-to-face interaction. However, even then, they were initially placed in different housing units within the prison, and though they were closer than they had been in years, direct contact remained limited. The anticipation of being able to reunite after so long made these final barriers almost unbearable. Yet, after years of setbacks, the end was in sight, and they clung to the hope that they would soon be allowed to see each other.

In April 2018, after further negotiations and internal processing, the long-awaited reunion finally occurred. Lyle and Erik were moved into the same housing unit within the facility, allowing them to interact freely during exercise, recreation, and meal times. The moment they saw each other, the years of isolation and separation seemed to dissolve, replaced by an overwhelming flood of relief and emotion. According to those who witnessed their reunion, both men broke down in tears, embracing each other in a way that only two brothers—bound not just by blood but by an extraordinary, shared tragedy—could. For Lyle and Erik, this was not just a reunion; it was a re-anchoring of their identities, a chance to reconnect with the only family they had left.

Their reunion provided a renewed sense of stability and emotional grounding. In the years following their reunion, both brothers continued to pursue their rehabilitative efforts, now bolstered by each other's presence. They became known within the prison as a team, often seen together, working on projects that served the inmate community, including educational programs and counseling support. The ability to lean on each other made their burdens a little lighter, providing a foundation of support that helped them navigate the challenges of prison life with a sense of unity.

The Menendez brothers' reunion became a source of interest and inspiration, even beyond the prison walls. Supporters viewed their reunion as a testament to the importance of family bonds, even in the bleakest of circumstances. Advocates for prison reform pointed to the brothers' case as an example of the positive impact family connections could have on inmates' mental health and rehabilitation. Their reunion was a rare glimpse of hope in a story marked by tragedy and loss—a reminder that, even in prison, human connections could foster resilience and personal growth.

For Lyle and Erik, the years apart had solidified their resolve, teaching them to endure isolation and hardship. Reunited, they were able to face the future with a renewed sense of purpose, finding strength in their shared history and mutual support. Their presence in each other's lives, after years of separation, served as a profound reminder that family could persist, even under the most challenging circumstances. Though they would never experience freedom as the outside world understood it, they had found a form of liberation in each other's company—a testament to the enduring power of familial love and the strength that could be drawn from even the simplest of human connections.

The Emotional Reunion at Richard J. Donovan Correctional Facility

The emotional reunion of Lyle and Erik Menendez at Richard J. Donovan Correctional Facility was a moment that, for the brothers, felt like the culmination of a lifetime of yearning and heartbreak. After nearly three decades of separation, where letters and brief, intermittent phone calls were the only means of connection, they were finally able to see each other in person, to speak without the barriers of distance, and to experience the comfort of their shared presence. For two men who had been inseparable in their early lives—bound not only by blood but by the extraordinary and traumatic events that had reshaped their family—this reunion represented both solace and a chance for healing.

The moment was raw and overwhelming. Witnesses described the reunion as filled with intense emotion; when Lyle and Erik finally came face-to-face, they embraced each other tightly, both breaking down into tears. This was more than just a reunion; it was the end of a long, painful journey of separation and the beginning of a new chapter where, even within the confines of a life sentence, they could support each other in ways that only family could. The depth of their shared experiences, from childhood memories to the dark events that led them to this place, surfaced in that instant. For both men, the reunion wasn't merely a comfort—it was a reminder that they were not alone in their struggles.

The emotional weight of the moment was compounded by the years they had spent grappling with their individual traumas in isolation. Lyle, the older brother, had always felt a sense of responsibility toward Erik, a need to protect him that lingered even through their imprisonment. For him, seeing Erik up close after so many years filled him with relief; despite the harsh realities of their shared fate, he could once again be there for his younger brother, physically present in a way that letters and phone calls could never replicate. Erik, who had suffered quietly, often consumed by guilt and the lingering shadows of their shared past, found a renewed sense of peace in Lyle's presence. Together, they could confront the weight of their memories and the complexities of their bond, no longer isolated in their grief.

As they settled into the reality of shared life within the prison, Lyle and Erik began to create a daily routine that allowed them to connect and support each other. They shared meals, exercised together, and found comfort in the regular, simple routines that prison life provided. Small moments, like talking over breakfast or sharing stories in the yard, became treasured rituals, a rhythm that brought familiarity and normalcy to a place defined by restriction and monotony. They often spent hours reflecting on their childhood, the choices that had led them to this point, and the complexities of their relationship with their parents. These conversations were not just about rehashing the past; they were part of a larger journey toward understanding and forgiveness, both of each other and of themselves.

Their reunion also had a noticeable impact on their emotional well-being. The presence of a trusted family member offered a reprieve from the relentless loneliness and emotional strain of incarceration. They were no longer navigating the darkness of prison life entirely alone; instead, they had each other as a source of strength and understanding. This newfound stability allowed both men to deepen their involvement in rehabilitative activities, finding purpose not only in self-reflection but in helping others within the prison. Lyle continued his work in inmate government and prison reform, while Erik remained dedicated to his educational and spiritual pursuits, including his work with terminally ill inmates. Their bond provided them with the emotional resilience needed to stay committed to these paths of personal growth.

The reunion also marked a turning point in how they were perceived within the prison community. Inmates and staff alike noted the profound connection between the brothers, a relationship that inspired a sense of respect. Their story, marked by tragedy and resilience, became a quiet example of the transformative power of family. For other inmates, many of whom lacked family connections or had been estranged from loved ones, the Menendez brothers' reunion underscored the importance of human connection, even within the bleak environment of a life sentence. In a place where survival often meant distancing oneself from vulnerability, Lyle and Erik's closeness showed that emotional support could coexist with strength and resilience.

Over time, their reunion became more than just an opportunity for companionship; it served as a foundation for mutual accountability and growth. They encouraged each other to maintain routines, to stay involved in constructive activities, and to focus on positive contributions to the prison community. Lyle, with his structured approach to leadership, often reminded Erik to keep pushing forward with his studies and spiritual growth. Erik, in turn, became a source of calm and introspection for Lyle, helping him navigate moments of frustration and reminding him of the progress they had made. Their relationship took on a deeper purpose, becoming a partnership dedicated to building meaning in an otherwise restricted life.

For the Menendez brothers, this reunion was more than a personal milestone; it was a profound affirmation of the enduring power of family and the possibility of resilience, even under the weight of a life sentence. Together, they faced the reality of their circumstances with renewed strength, finding moments of solace and connection amidst the relentless structure of prison life. Their reunion didn't erase their past, nor did it soften the enormity of the crime that had led them here. But it provided them with a foundation, a shared hope that allowed them to confront each day with dignity and, perhaps, a semblance of peace. In the years following their reunion, Lyle and Erik continued to walk side by side, navigating the routines of prison life with the understanding that, for as long as they were allowed, they would have each other. They found a way to be family again, not in the traditional sense but in a manner that spoke to the depth of their bond and the resilience of the human spirit. In the confined, regulated world of prison, their relationship remained a bright spot, a symbol of continuity that offered a measure of comfort and purpose. Their reunion, though modest in the scale of the world outside, became an act of redemption in its own quiet way—a chance to live out their sentences not as two separate individuals, but as brothers, standing together in the face of a shared, unchanging fate.

Part VI: Renewed Hope

Chapter 10: New Evidence and Public Interest

Roy Rosselló's Allegations Against José Menendez

The story of the Menendez brothers had seemed all but settled. Lyle and Erik Menendez, convicted in the sensational 1996 trial for the murder of their parents, were serving life sentences without the possibility of parole. Public interest had waxed and waned over the decades, stirred now and then by media retrospectives or true crime documentaries that dissected every angle of the case. But for most, the narrative was fixed: two privileged sons who killed their parents, with murky claims of abuse and trauma never fully corroborated. That is, until an unexpected voice emerged from the shadows—one that rekindled the debate, raised haunting questions, and cast José Menendez, their father, in a new, sinister light.

In 2023, Roy Rosselló, a former member of the wildly popular Puerto Rican boy band Menudo, made headlines with disturbing allegations. Rosselló claimed that he, too, had been a victim of José Menendez's abuse. According to Rosselló, José had sexually assaulted him when he was a teenager in the 1980s, during a period when Menendez was an executive at RCA Records, responsible for the success of major artists, including Menudo. Rosselló's story, shocking in its own right, carried an even heavier weight because it seemed to corroborate the abuse claims that Lyle and Erik had maintained throughout their trials. His voice, one from outside the insular world of the Menendez family, added an unsettling new dimension to the brothers' narrative—a validation of trauma that the justice system had largely dismissed.

For those familiar with the Menudo phenomenon, Rosselló's allegations felt like an intrusion into the glossy, manufactured image of youthful innocence and boyish charm that the band represented. In the 1980s, Menudo was an international sensation, a group of teenage boys whose carefully curated image captivated audiences worldwide. But behind the scenes, Menudo's young members were subjected to grueling schedules, strict management, and, as Rosselló now alleged, a far darker reality. In his account, José Menendez had used his position of power and influence to exploit him, creating an environment where Rosselló felt vulnerable and trapped. For him, coming forward was not only a personal reckoning but also an attempt to find justice for trauma he had long buried.

When news of Rosselló's allegations broke, it reignited public interest in the Menendez case. Supporters of Lyle and Erik saw this revelation as a vindication, a chilling confirmation of the abuse claims that had been central to their defense decades earlier. Suddenly, what had once been dismissed as unsubstantiated allegations became part of a broader, more disturbing pattern. If José Menendez had been capable of preying on Rosselló, an outsider, could it not be plausible that his own sons had suffered similar abuse in the privacy of their family home? This new evidence reopened the question of whether Lyle and Erik's crime was the desperate act of two young men who had reached a breaking point after years of exploitation and fear.

For others, Rosselló's allegations introduced an uncomfortable layer of complexity to an already fraught story. The Menendez case had always been polarizing, dividing public opinion between those who saw the brothers as entitled killers and those who believed their claims of self-defense rooted in prolonged abuse. Rosselló's testimony blurred these lines further, complicating the public's understanding of José Menendez and the possible motivations behind the crime. The man who had once been cast as a strict but successful father—a figure of the American Dream gone awry—was now, in the eyes of many, a potential predator whose power and influence may have masked a hidden darkness. The neatly packaged narrative of family tragedy and greed began to unravel, exposing a much more disturbing tapestry of trauma, silence, and buried secrets.

Rosselló's decision to speak out was not without personal cost. He risked public scrutiny, backlash, and the reopening of painful memories. Yet, he felt a sense of duty, a need to tell his story and shed light on the aspects of José Menendez's life that had been hidden for so long.

In interviews, Rosselló spoke of the fear and confusion he experienced as a young boy, caught in the grip of a powerful man who held sway over his career and future. His testimony was raw and painful, resonating with an authenticity that was difficult to dismiss. His voice, vulnerable yet resolute, became a catalyst, breathing new life into a case that had once seemed consigned to history. The media quickly picked up on Rosselló's allegations, and soon his story was everywhere—covered by news outlets, analyzed in podcasts, and dissected in forums dedicated to true crime. For many, his account was a revelation, a chilling corroboration of what they had always suspected. For others, it raised troubling questions about the limits of the justice system and the importance of understanding trauma in its many complex forms. As Rosselló's allegations continued to spread, there was renewed public pressure to reexamine the Menendez brothers' case, to consider whether the narrative of their crime was incomplete and if justice had truly been served. Amid this renewed attention, legal experts and advocates began to speak out, calling for a review of the Menendez brothers' convictions. They argued that the criminal justice system had failed to fully consider the psychological impact of abuse, especially in cases where victims felt trapped and powerless. Lyle and Erik's initial claims of abuse had been viewed skeptically, filtered through the lens of a high-stakes, media-driven trial. But now, with an outsider's voice affirming their narrative, there was a growing sense that perhaps, in the quest for accountability, the courts had overlooked a deeper truth—a truth that was now, years later, coming to light.

For the Menendez brothers, locked away for life, Rosselló's allegations were both a painful reminder and a glimmer of hope. The accusations forced them to relive the trauma they had long struggled to articulate, bringing memories of their father's control, manipulation, and alleged abuse back into sharp focus. Yet, Rosselló's testimony also represented a form of validation, a small but significant acknowledgment that they had not suffered alone, and that their voices, silenced for so long, might finally be heard with the gravity they deserved.

In the wake of Rosselló's allegations, questions loomed over the Menendez brothers' case. Could this new evidence lead to a reexamination of their trial, or perhaps even a reconsideration of their sentences? Would the world finally understand the complexities that had shaped their lives, and by extension, the desperation that may have driven them to commit such an unspeakable act? The answers remained uncertain, but what was clear was that the Menendez story was far from over. Rosselló's courage in sharing his painful past had reignited a dialogue, casting a shadow over the legacy of José Menendez and forcing the public to confront a harrowing reality that had long been buried under the weight of scandal and spectacle.

The narrative that had once seemed straightforward—a story of two privileged sons turning on their parents out of greed—was now layered with unsettling implications. Rosselló's allegations invited the world to consider the hidden lives, the untold stories, and the buried truths that lay beneath the polished surfaces of power and success. And as the public revisited the Menendez case with this new evidence, a different story began to take shape—a story of survival, trauma, and the lengths to which individuals will go to escape the darkness of abuse. The Menendez brothers, though forever marked by their crime, became part of a larger conversation, one that questioned the very nature of justice and the role of compassion in understanding even the most horrific acts.

Erik's Letter: A Cry for Help

In 2018, a letter from Erik Menendez surfaced, casting a haunting light on the Menendez brothers' claims of abuse and reawakening the painful narrative they had tried to articulate decades before. Written in 1988, a year before the murders of their parents, the letter was addressed to Erik's cousin, Andy Cano. In it, Erik described in raw, desperate terms the torment he was enduring at the hands of his father, José Menendez. This letter, filled with fear and helplessness, became a chilling piece of evidence that seemed to support the brothers' defense—a cry for help that had gone unheeded, a glimpse into a private nightmare that would later end in tragedy.

The contents of Erik's letter were heartbreaking, revealing a young man trapped in a cycle of abuse, unable to see a way out. He wrote to his cousin in hopes of finding someone who would understand, someone who might offer him some measure of comfort or guidance. "I've been trying to avoid dad," Erik wrote, his words trembling with the weight of fear and shame. "It's still happening,

Andy, but it's worse for me now... I never know when it's going to happen, and it's driving me crazy. Every night, I stay up thinking he might come in." The letter conveyed an acute sense of dread, the kind that only someone living in constant terror could understand. This wasn't the voice of a rebellious teenager but of a young man reaching out from the depths of despair, his vulnerability laid bare in ink.

For those who had doubted the brothers' claims of abuse, Erik's letter forced a reconsideration. Here was a tangible record, written long before any legal battles, that seemed to corroborate the horrific details that had been presented during the trials. The letter painted a vivid picture of Erik's state of mind—a young man psychologically crushed by his father's alleged abuse, uncertain and fearful about what each day might bring. It showed the toll that constant fear and emotional manipulation had taken on him, eroding his ability to think beyond survival and filling him with a sense of isolation so profound that even his own family did not seem able to protect him.

The release of the letter also raised troubling questions about the adults in Erik's life, those who may have been aware of the abuse yet felt powerless or unwilling to intervene. Andy Cano, to whom the letter was addressed, had testified during the trial that Erik had confided in him about the abuse, sharing stories of incidents that no young person should ever experience. However, for reasons still unclear, Cano had not acted upon this knowledge beyond offering Erik a sympathetic ear. Erik's letter exposed a painful reality often faced by victims of abuse: the reluctance, fear, or disbelief of those who might have intervened but instead turned a blind eye, leaving the victim alone with their suffering.

For Erik, writing that letter may have been an act of desperation—a final attempt to reach out before surrendering to the reality that there was no escape from his father's grip. The letter carried a plea for understanding and, possibly, for intervention, but it also hinted at his diminishing hope. There was a quiet resignation in his words, an acceptance of his fate that spoke to the profound psychological toll that years of alleged abuse had taken on him. Erik's young mind, overwhelmed by the burden of these experiences, had seemingly reached a breaking point long before the fateful night that would change his life forever.

In the context of the Menendez trial, this letter took on an almost haunting significance. Had it been found sooner, it might have altered the course of their defense, offering a level of validation that could have swayed public opinion and perhaps even the jury's decision. But in the 1990s, this letter remained buried—forgotten, unread, and undiscovered in the tangled web of family secrets and trauma. It wasn't until years later that it surfaced, its words untouched by the complexities of courtroom strategy or public scrutiny, standing as a testament to the brothers' suffering long before the events that would ultimately lead them to murder.

The letter's discovery sparked fresh discussions about the intersection of abuse and justice. Advocates for trauma-informed approaches within the legal system saw Erik's letter as an emblem of how abuse often goes unseen or ignored, especially when it involves powerful individuals.

They argued that cases like the Menendez brothers' highlighted the need for a more compassionate understanding of trauma and its profound psychological effects. Erik's letter, they contended, was a cry for help that society failed to answer—an opportunity lost, with tragic consequences.

For Erik himself, the letter's release must have been a bittersweet moment. He was still behind bars, serving a life sentence, but the letter gave voice to a past he had been forced to relive, over and over, throughout his imprisonment. It was a piece of evidence that validated his claims, yet it could not undo the crime he had committed or bring back the lives lost. The letter served as a reminder of the horrors he had endured, but also of the consequences that followed when no help came. It was a cruel irony: the one piece of his truth that might have offered some measure of understanding had arrived too late to change his fate.

The public reaction to Erik's letter was mixed. For some, it confirmed what they had long suspected—that the Menendez brothers had acted out of desperation, driven to their breaking point by years of unrelenting abuse. For others, the letter was a painful reminder of the complexity of trauma, offering a window into a world of suffering that many would rather not see. Yet, there were still those who remained unmoved, convinced that the brothers' actions were inexcusable regardless of their past. But for Erik and Lyle, the letter was a moment of quiet vindication, a sliver of understanding that, while too late to change their sentences, offered some validation for the years they had spent pleading their truth.

Erik's letter also became a powerful symbol in the ongoing conversation about abuse and the criminal justice system. It illuminated the dark corners where abuse often hides, undetected and unaddressed, until it manifests in tragedy. Advocates called for greater awareness, for systems of support that could intervene before trauma reached such catastrophic ends. Erik's letter, with its stark honesty and vulnerability, became more than just a document from a lost past—it was a rallying cry for a more compassionate approach to justice, a reminder that beneath every headline lies a human story, complex and painful, deserving of understanding.

In the quiet solitude of his cell, Erik may have reflected on that letter, the words of a young man desperate for escape and understanding, penned in a moment of vulnerability that would only be fully recognized years later. It was a cry for help that had fallen silent in the noise of sensational headlines and public opinion, but now it stood as a piece of his truth—a small fragment of the pain and fear that had shaped his life. Though it came too late to change his fate, the letter offered a sliver of hope that, perhaps one day, his story might be seen in its full, tragic complexity.

Netflix, TikTok, and the Menendez Brothers' Resurgence in Media

In the past few years, the Menendez brothers' story has experienced an unexpected resurgence, fueled by modern media platforms like Netflix and TikTok. Once relegated to the annals of '90s true crime, their case has found a new audience among younger generations, thanks to streaming documentaries and viral TikTok videos that revisit the story with a fresh perspective. This resurgence has reignited public fascination, but it has also reframed the conversation surrounding Lyle and Erik Menendez, casting their actions and alleged motivations in a more empathetic light as society grows increasingly sensitive to issues of trauma, abuse, and mental health.

In 2021, Netflix's true crime documentary series *The Menendez Murders: Erik Tells All* provided a platform for Erik Menendez to share his experiences and retell the story from his perspective, shining a spotlight on the abuse allegations that had been central to the brothers' defense. Through candid interviews and re-enactments, the series presented a more nuanced view of the events leading up to the murders, emphasizing the complex family dynamics and the allegations of abuse that the brothers claimed had driven them to their breaking point. This retelling, without the pressure of a courtroom or the sensationalism of '90s media, allowed audiences to connect with the brothers' narrative in a way that had previously been overshadowed by the spectacle of their trial.

Netflix's documentary series reignited public interest, especially among younger viewers who had not experienced the case firsthand in the '90s. The series painted a picture of two young men who, despite their privileged upbringing, suffered from what they described as years of trauma inflicted by their father. For a generation that has grown up with more awareness of mental health issues and the impact of trauma, the story resonated deeply. Audiences began to see the brothers not merely as the infamous killers in a shocking crime story but as possible victims of unchecked abuse, reacting out of desperation in a situation that they felt had no other escape.

This renewed narrative quickly spread to TikTok, where true crime content has a substantial following. TikTok users, particularly those in their teens and early twenties, began creating videos that analyzed the Menendez case, discussed the allegations of abuse, and examined court footage with fresh eyes. In these short, digestible video clips, users dissected the body language of Lyle and Erik during their trial, debated the credibility of their abuse claims, and revisited the notorious 911 call placed on the night of the murders. Many TikTok creators used these videos to advocate for a re-evaluation of the Menendez brothers' case, pointing to the evolving understanding of trauma and abuse as a reason to reexamine their sentences. What began as a niche interest on TikTok quickly gained traction, as hashtags like #MenendezBrothers and #JusticeForMenendez trended, garnering millions of views. This new wave of interest didn't just bring attention back to the case; it generated a movement. TikTok creators and their followers called for a reassessment of the brothers' trial, suggesting that the courts had overlooked the severe impact of abuse on Lyle and Erik's mental states. Many argued that if the trial were held today, the defense would likely receive more weight, as modern legal and psychological perspectives on abuse have advanced considerably since the ‘90s. The brothers’ sentences were viewed by some as a reflection of an era that misunderstood trauma, one that saw their claims as an attempt to dodge accountability rather than as an honest depiction of the horrifying conditions they endured.

The TikTok movement gained enough attention that mainstream media outlets took notice, publishing articles that explored the Menendez brothers’ newfound popularity among Gen Z and the reasons behind it. This resurgence highlighted how perspectives on crime and punishment have shifted, with society now more willing to consider the psychological impact of trauma, especially when it comes to cases involving alleged abuse within families. The Menendez brothers, once seen as symbols of greed and entitlement, became, for many, symbols of the failure of the justice system to protect victims of abuse and to understand the nuances of trauma.

This new framing was further amplified by the stories of other individuals coming forward with similar experiences of alleged abuse by José Menendez, most notably Roy Rosselló, a former member of the boy band Menudo, who claimed that José had sexually abused him as a teenager. Rosselló's allegations lent further credence to Lyle and Erik's accounts, supporting their narrative and underscoring the possibility that their actions were born from profound suffering and desperation. His story, combined with the growing advocacy on platforms like TikTok, created a renewed sense of urgency around the case. What had once been a closed chapter was now being re-opened in the court of public opinion, with younger audiences calling for a reassessment of the brothers' life sentences.

As this cultural movement grew, the Menendez brothers began to be viewed through a more compassionate lens. Platforms like TikTok allowed people to engage with the story in a personal and emotional way, making the Menendez case a conversation about justice, empathy, and the complex consequences of trauma. Some TikTok creators went so far as to start petitions advocating for the brothers' release or a re-trial, arguing that the justice system of the '90s had been ill-equipped to handle a case that involved allegations of prolonged familial abuse. These petitions, though unlikely to directly affect the legal system, highlighted the changing perceptions around the case and emphasized a collective desire to see justice not as black-and-white but as a spectrum that considers the full breadth of human experience.

The resurgence of interest on TikTok and Netflix has not only affected public opinion but also potentially influenced legal advocates and family members of the brothers, who are working to bring the case back into the courts. Lawyers familiar with the case have discussed the possibility of re-examining it in light of today's understanding of trauma and abuse. In May 2023, the Menendez brothers filed a petition for a new evidentiary hearing, citing Rosselló's allegations and Erik's 1988 letter as key evidence that might warrant a re-evaluation of their sentences. The attention garnered by Netflix and TikTok has undoubtedly added weight to these legal efforts, bringing the case back into the spotlight and reminding the public that, despite the passage of time, some stories remain unresolved.

In many ways, the Menendez brothers' resurgence in the media has transformed them from infamous figures of true crime lore into complex symbols of how society's understanding of trauma and justice has evolved. Platforms like Netflix and TikTok have allowed audiences to engage with their story in a multi-dimensional way, blending factual recounting with emotional empathy. For those who grew up hearing about the Menendez case as a tale of greed and patricide, this renewed attention has provided a lens that offers nuance, context, and, perhaps, a deeper understanding of what might have driven two young men to commit such an unfathomable act.

As the Menendez brothers' story continues to evolve in the public eye, it serves as a reminder that the past is never fully static. Modern media has brought their story to life once again, inviting fresh scrutiny and re-opening old wounds. What was once considered a closed case now serves as a living narrative that challenges society's perceptions of guilt, punishment, and the complexities of family trauma. Whether or not this resurgence will lead to any legal reconsideration remains to be seen, but one thing is clear: through Netflix, TikTok, and the unyielding power of collective curiosity, the Menendez brothers' story has become more than just a crime—it has become a reflection of society's evolving understanding of justice, empathy, and the hidden scars that often lie beneath the surface.

The November Court Hearing: Hopes and Expectations

The upcoming November court hearing has become a beacon of hope for Lyle and Erik Menendez and their supporters, signaling a potential turning point in a case that has haunted the brothers—and captivated the public—for over three decades. Scheduled to review new evidence and reconsider their sentences, this hearing represents not only a rare legal opportunity for the Menendez brothers but also a symbolic moment in the broader conversation about justice, trauma, and the evolving understanding of abuse within the American legal system. For those who believe the brothers were acting out of desperation rather than malice, the November hearing has sparked cautious optimism that the system may finally offer them a chance at a revised sentence and, perhaps, even freedom.

The November hearing is set to consider the impact of recently surfaced evidence, particularly the allegations from former Menudo band member Roy Rosselló and

Erik's 1988 letter to his cousin Andy, in which he detailed his fear and anxiety surrounding his father's alleged abuse. Both pieces of evidence provide a corroborative framework that the brothers' original defense team could only speculate on during the 1996 trials. Supporters argue that this new evidence paints a far more compelling picture of the environment of abuse, manipulation, and control that Lyle and Erik endured under their father, José Menendez. For many, these revelations have added depth to the narrative, suggesting that the brothers' actions were not driven by greed, as prosecutors had once claimed, but by a breaking point reached after years of alleged trauma and hopelessness.

As the hearing approaches, the brothers' legal team is working to frame this new evidence as pivotal to understanding the psychological state Lyle and Erik were in at the time of the murders. They plan to argue that if the court had access to these corroborating testimonies and the letter at the original trial, the narrative might have been very different. With modern psychological insights into trauma and abuse now recognized by the courts in ways that were less common in the '90s, the defense hopes to present a case that contextualizes the murders within a framework of prolonged psychological distress, rather than cold-blooded malice. The legal strategy centers on emphasizing how the absence of these insights during the original trial created a biased view of the brothers' actions, one that painted them as privileged killers rather than victims of abuse who acted out of desperation.

Public expectations surrounding the hearing are as high as they are divided. For many, particularly the younger generation who have come to view the case through the lens of Netflix documentaries and TikTok discussions, the hearing is a long-overdue moment for reconsideration. This group sees the potential for a revised sentence as a reflection of society's evolving understanding of abuse and the importance of viewing such cases with a trauma-informed lens. Supporters of the Menendez brothers, many of whom are vocal on social media, hope the court will acknowledge the weight of the new evidence, if not as a means for total exoneration, then at least to reconsider the harshness of a life sentence without parole. They see this hearing as a chance for justice to be redefined—not in black-and-white terms, but in a way that accounts for the complexities of the human experience and the profound impact of unresolved trauma.

However, there are also voices of skepticism and opposition. Some members of the public, including families of victims of violent crimes, argue that the Menendez brothers' crimes should not be excused, regardless of any alleged abuse. For them, the murders remain an unthinkable betrayal of familial bonds, and the brothers' life sentences serve as a necessary consequence for their actions. This faction fears that revisiting the case with a more lenient perspective could set a concerning precedent, one that might enable future perpetrators to evade accountability by claiming abuse. This perspective underscores the ongoing tension between calls for justice reform and the need to uphold consequences for severe crimes, a debate that will likely continue to loom large as the hearing unfolds.

For Lyle and Erik themselves, the hearing carries a deeply personal weight. After years of enduring the emotional strain of life sentences, the possibility of a revised sentence offers a glimmer of hope—a chance to escape the seemingly endless monotony of prison life and perhaps even reintegrate into society. Both brothers have changed significantly during their decades of incarceration, with each dedicating himself to personal growth, rehabilitation, and supporting other inmates. The prospect of parole or even a reduced sentence would allow them to step into a world they have only glimpsed through prison walls since their early twenties, giving them an opportunity to live out their later years with a sense of freedom they once thought permanently lost.

The hearing will also likely delve into the impact that incarceration has had on both brothers. Legal experts and psychologists involved in the case are expected to present assessments of how the brothers have evolved over time and whether they would pose any threat to society if released. Testimonies from those who have observed Lyle and Erik's conduct in prison are expected to reinforce the narrative that they have worked to rehabilitate themselves, contributing positively to the prison community. These testimonies will likely emphasize their commitment to constructive paths, such as Lyle's involvement in prison governance and reform initiatives and Erik's dedication to educational programs and supporting terminally ill inmates. By focusing on their development and redemption, the defense aims to present them not as the individuals who committed the crime in 1989 but as men who have, in many ways, transcended their past actions through meaningful change.

In the legal community, this hearing has garnered significant interest as a case study in evolving justice practices. Legal scholars, psychologists, and advocates for trauma-informed justice are watching closely, viewing the Menendez case as a potential landmark moment in the acknowledgment of abuse as a mitigating factor in sentencing. Many hope that this hearing will signal a shift toward a more compassionate judicial approach, one that considers the full scope of an individual's life circumstances before rendering a verdict that will shape their entire future. Should the hearing result in a revised sentence, it could pave the way for broader changes in how the legal system addresses cases involving trauma, creating a precedent for more nuanced sentencing considerations in the future.

As the hearing date approaches, emotions run high. For Lyle and Erik, this may be the last opportunity to present their case with the full weight of the new evidence in their favor. They have spent the past several years preparing for this moment, investing their hope in the possibility that the legal system might finally acknowledge their version of events—a version not based solely on sensationalism and courtroom drama but on the quiet, painful realities of abuse and survival. They approach the hearing with a cautious optimism, aware of the challenges but also buoyed by the support that has grown around their case in recent years.

Ultimately, the outcome of the November hearing is uncertain, and much remains in the hands of the judicial system. However, the significance of this moment extends beyond Lyle and Erik's personal fate. The hearing represents a pivotal point in society's ongoing dialogue about justice, trauma, and redemption. Whether or not their sentences are revised, the Menendez brothers' case has already sparked a larger conversation about how the law should reckon with the complexities of human behavior, particularly when it intersects with issues of family, abuse, and psychological turmoil.

As the day of the hearing approaches, supporters, skeptics, and onlookers alike hold their breath, waiting to see if the court will embrace this chance for reflection and, perhaps, a measure of mercy. For now, Lyle and Erik can only wait, knowing that this hearing holds their last, best hope for freedom—a freedom that, if granted, would be tempered by the scars of their past but, at long last, would allow them to start anew outside the prison walls.

Conclusion

The Menendez brothers' story has always been one of contrasts—a privileged upbringing against a backdrop of alleged abuse, a life of opportunity overshadowed by familial dysfunction, and an ultimate act of violence that continues to polarize public opinion. What began as a shocking crime in 1989 has evolved into a complex narrative about family, trauma, and the limitations of the justice system. As society gains a deeper understanding of the psychological impact of abuse, the Menendez brothers' case serves as a prism through which we can reflect on the nuances of justice and redemption.

In retrospect, the Menendez case is a tragic reminder of how secrets and unaddressed trauma can fester within families, creating fault lines that, when left unchecked, erupt in unimaginable ways. José and Kitty Menendez appeared to embody the American Dream, achieving success, prestige, and power, yet behind closed doors, their family was haunted by a darkness that remained hidden from the outside world. Lyle and Erik's trial brought their personal horrors into public view, though their stories of abuse were dismissed by many as fabrications. Over the decades, however, new evidence and shifting cultural attitudes toward abuse have shed light on the validity of their claims, raising questions about whether justice was truly served.

For Lyle and Erik, decades of incarceration have offered little solace but have allowed them the space to seek redemption. Through their rehabilitation efforts and advocacy work within the prison system, they have transformed themselves from symbols of infamy into men striving to make a positive impact. Lyle's leadership in inmate government and prison reform, as well as Erik's support for terminally ill inmates and his dedication to spiritual growth, demonstrate a commitment to personal change and social responsibility. Their work reflects a quiet resilience—a choice to build a new purpose within the confines of a life sentence. Despite the weight of their past, they have found ways to help others, whether by guiding younger inmates, supporting fellow abuse survivors, or advocating for changes within the prison community.

Beyond their personal transformations, the Menendez brothers have also become unwitting advocates for abuse survivors. Their story resonates with individuals who have experienced similar traumas, offering a rare perspective on the hidden scars that abuse can leave. In recent years, their case has inspired discussions about trauma-informed justice and the importance of understanding the psychological toll that abuse can take. By sharing their experiences, Lyle and Erik have contributed to a broader conversation about the ways in which unacknowledged trauma can shape actions, often with tragic consequences. They have inspired advocates and legal scholars to reconsider how the justice system handles cases involving abuse, pushing for an approach that recognizes the complexity of human behavior and the influence of past trauma.

The legacy of the Menendez brothers is as complex as the story itself. On one hand, they are remembered as the perpetrators of a brutal crime, a cautionary tale of wealth, privilege, and the destructive power of unchecked family dysfunction. On the other hand, they represent the potential for growth, resilience, and the possibility of reform, even within the harshest of circumstances. Their story has evolved into a reflection of society's changing perspectives on trauma, accountability, and the need for empathy in the face of unimaginable pain. While their actions can never be justified, the Menendez brothers' journey has offered a stark reminder that behind every crime lies a story—one that often reveals as much about society's failures as it does about individual choices.

Today, the Menendez brothers' story serves not only as a reflection on the past but also as a call for reform. It invites society to question the structures that fail to protect abuse survivors, the stigmas that surround trauma, and the rigidity of a justice system that often overlooks the profound effects of psychological suffering. As advocates continue to push for trauma-informed approaches within the legal system, the Menendez brothers' case remains a powerful example of why empathy and understanding are essential components of true justice.

Ultimately, the Menendez case will be remembered as a tragedy—a story of lives destroyed by violence, secrets, and suffering. Yet, within that tragedy, there is also a legacy of resilience, a testament to the strength of the human spirit, even in the darkest of circumstances. For Lyle and Erik, their journey may never lead to freedom in the traditional sense, but through their advocacy and efforts at rehabilitation, they have forged a new path—one that reflects their commitment to growth, accountability, and the hope of making a difference in the lives of others. In this way, the Menendez brothers' story transcends its origins, transforming from a tale of loss and despair into one of redemption, reform, and, ultimately, a quiet but enduring impact on the world they once left behind.

Made in United States
Troutdale, OR
12/02/2024